THIS BOOK IS PART OF

THE SIDNEY ROSENBLATT (CLC'82)

HOLOCAUST COLLECTION

AT

FORDHAM UNIVERSITY LIBRARIES

AS LONG AS I REMAIN ALIVE

"Auschwitz, Auschwitz
I cannot forget you
As long as I remain alive..."
(from a prison song)

In loving memory of my parents, Elias and Rosette Rodriguez Garcia, and my sister, Sippora.

AS LONG AS I REMAIN ALIVE

by

Max Rodriguez Garcia

as told to

Priscilla Alden Garcia

A PORTALS BOOK

COPYRIGHT © 1979 BY MAX RODRIGUEZ GARCIA

FIRST EDITION

ALL RIGHTS RESERVED. EXCEPT FOR BRIEF QUOTATIONS IN A REVIEW, THE AUTHOR'S ORIGINAL TEXT, OR PARTS THEREOF, MUST NOT BE REPRODUCED IN ANY FORM WITHOUT PERMISSION IN WRITING FROM THE PUBLISHER. FOR INFORMATION, ADDRESS PORTALS PRESS, P.O. BOX 1048, TUSCALOOSA, AL 35401.

LIBRARY OF CONGRESS CARD CATALOG NO. 78-65309

ISBN 0-916620-25-5

MANUFACTURED IN THE UNITED STATES OF AMERICA

CONTENTS

Preface

Acknowledgment

Part 1	1945	1
Part 2	A Dutch Jewish Family of Diamond Workers	35
Part 3	The Camps	79
	Buna, 1943	81
	Auschwitz, 1943	85
	Auschwitz, 1944	93
	The Paketstelle Kommando, 1944	103
	A Last Transport from Auschwitz, January 1945	114
	Mauthausen, Melk, and March to Ebensee February, March 1945	120
Part 4	Serving American Forces in Europe	125
	The 319th Infantry Regiment, 1945—1946	127
	The C.I.C., 1946	139
	Summer, 1946	150
	September, 1946	159
Part 5	The Immigrant	165
Part 6	Taking Root	199

Dedicated to Arthur H. and Jean Clark, who sponsored my immigration to the United States.

Preface

Like the Ancient Mariner, Max Garcia has often tried to buttonhole a friend and make him listen to some small part of the story of what happened to him, a Dutch Sephardic Jew, as a result of Nazi policy in World War II. Whenever he is asked, he talks to classroom students about his experiences in Nazi concentration camps. Many listeners are taken aback or are a little embarrassed. Few invite him to elaborate. The subject does not qualify as polite conversation. Most of us Americans have not concerned ourselves with the implications of the Holocaust. On several occasions, however, Max has met and talked with fellow concentration camp survivors, and their conversations have lasted for hours—grim, soul-searching exchanges. No one seems to question that the survivors should carry this burden.

Almost four years ago Max and I sat down to begin taping sessions of his recollections. We wanted the children to have an honest account, when they were mature enough to read it, of what happened to Max's family, and to him. We wanted them to know how a man could become as cunning as his tormentors in order to survive his planned death at Nazi hands as well as years of persecution and degradation as a Jew. We wanted them to understand the confusion of a young man trying to apply his camp survival education in a peacetime world that could not use it. We wanted them to know about terror so great that their father chose to hide from his Jewish heritage for many years. We wanted them to understand how their father gradually came to realize his individual worth in American society, how he came to renew his commitment to Judaism, and what he then went through to carry out his lifetime dream of becoming a practicing architect. Yet we wanted to convey that coming to terms with the Holocaust has been and will continue to be a lifetime effort.

The emerging manuscript appeared to have much to say to many people, not just our family. Though Max took no notes as a young man, he proved to have an excellent memory of events and experiences that educated him. After the dictating, we did hours of back-up research. We read many sources and learned a great deal more than young Max knew as a participant in one significant phase of modern Western history. However, this account relates only Max's personal recollections. Except as Max and his family saw and were affected by events, we have not attempted to interpret the history of the German occupation of Holland, or of the concentration camp system, or of the American occupation following Germany's defeat.

Much has been said about the Holocaust, and yet enough will never be said. Perhaps Max's account will motivate readers to seek out other accounts or scholarly studies. Max mentions in the last chapter that there are other human conflagrations that have devastated and, to this day, are gobbling up thousands of lives in various countries of the world. Few free people are interested. The citizens of established democratic societies tend to take their privileges for granted.

Priscilla Alden Garcia
San Francisco, California

ACKNOWLEDGMENT

We want to thank Max Knight, recently retired principal editor of University of California press, for his patient guidance and advice through various stages of the manuscript. He was our mentor in story development and knowledgeable editor of our European historical material.

Max and Priscilla Garcia

* * * * * * *

It is unusual for a person credited in an acknowledgment to respond. Yet there seems to be no other place in this book to draw attention to the extraordinary devotion and empathy of a wife who spent years in patiently encouraging her husband to record this story.

Max Knight

PART 1

1945

Max R. Garcia, wearing Dutch flag patch, as aide to First Battalion, 319th Infantry Regiment of the 80th Infantry Division, U.S. Army, 1945.

I

* *365. The 3d Squadron moved into the zone at 0605 on this date [May 6, 1945] and immediately advanced south reporting no enemy resistance of any kind. Here again PW's surrendered in droves and occupied much of the area. At 100 A Troop forward elements entered the town of EBENSEE and reported that a concentration camp was located in that town. Further investigation proved that the camp contained 16,000 starving political prisoners and that the conditions in the camp were deplorable. As many as three hundred were dying every day from starvation and unattended diseases. They lived in filth and stench [and] were at a stage where eating their own dead was the sane thing to do. The camp compared easily with BUCHENWALD or ORDHRUF [OHRDRUF]. Immediate action was taken by the Group Commander, who examined the camp and requested food and medical attention for the indescribable scene. While food and medics were on route, the men of the 3d Squadron did whatever possible to ease the situation. They took estimates of the sick and dying and decided what would be needed to treat them, feed that [sic] and evaluate them. The information they compiled and the preliminary work that they did was a great help toward the final rehabilitation of the prisoners.*

Crowding the fence and listening intently, we heard them on the road below. An unfamiliar rumbling that we had not heard before. We saw their dust rising from the valley. The rumbling, squeaking sound of their climb up our road grew louder with their approach; then two enormous tanks lumbered into view around the bend of our road, followed by a curious, small, open vehicle. On

---
* *After-Action Report, 3d Cavalry Group, Mechanized, 9 August 1944 to May 1945.* p. 90.

our side of the fence, we prisoners surged toward the locked main gate as the tanks and auxiliary vehicle slowly pulled to a halt just outside.

Soldiers in unfamiliar uniforms peered in frank amazement from the tops of the tanks at a mass of shrunken, ghastly scarecrows in filthy, striped rags, a reeking mass with heads shaved except for a center stripe. The soldiers stared at us and we stared at them.

Two old *Volkswehr* stood trembling and silent but still at their posts outside the gate. Too old to serve in the German Army, these men did service as homeguardsmen in their village of Ebensee. Suddenly a soldier leaned down from the nearest tank, yanked the rifle out of the hands of the *Volkswehr* at the right side of the gate, broke it over the gun turret, and hung it over the gate to our camp. That thrilling crack still resounds in my memory.

The day, I was to learn later, was the 6th of May, 1945, a Sunday. It was midday.

The silence of the first shock of our encounter now broken, the gates somehow were opened, and we drew back to allow the roaring tanks and their small escort to roll slowly into the middle of our barren *Appellplatz*. Prisoners swarmed around as the engines switched off. The soldiers in and on the tanks seemed afraid. They looked as if they did not care to come down among us. They may have been fresh from the latest battles, but we appeared to be too much for them. These hungry eyes. These sunken faces and skeletal bodies. These stinking subhumans. Us!

Some of us tried to climb onto the tanks but were politely rebuffed with hand gestures. Standing among the crowd of prisoners around the tanks, I watched a soldier take out a pack of Lucky Strikes and light a cigarette. Now these were American cigarettes, I knew, for I had seen just such cigarettes back in Holland and even advertised in English-language papers and magazines my father had brought me, insisting that I learn some English. So these were American forces!

"It's been a long time since I had a Lucky Strike," I yelled up over the din to the soldier. He looked down in surprise, singling me out. "You speak English?" In my daring I answered, "Yes." "Well, come on up here." He reached down to give me a hand up onto the tank. Once there I was given that Lucky and the soldier lit it for me. I took a long pull, inhaling deeply. The sea of faces on the *Appellplatz* reeled. I had become accustomed to smoking what I thought was strong stuff, such as tree bark and brown wrapping paper, but the American cigarette made me dizzy. I braced myself, then switched my smoking method to an occasional cautious puff. Meanwhile the soldier was pelting me with questions. Signalling him to slow down, I struggled to understand and to answer with single words or gestures. What was my name? Where was I from? What was I doing here? How many prisoners were in this camp? What were they doing here? Where did they come from? I had very few knowledgeable answers, but we worked hard at exchanging information with my few words of English and many hand signs. The American spoke no other languages. For my part, I asked if the war was over, and, more or less, what was going on. The Nazis, I learned, had not yet officially surrendered but surrender was expected at any moment. A report of Hitler's death had been confirmed.

The soldier radioed to his headquarters that our camp had been opened and that a prisoner who spoke a little English had been found. My soldier friend, I noted, was a sergeant, and apparently in command of the small tank force liberating our camp. I set about trying to persuade him to come down and take a look around. He was hesitant but he and a soldier companion were eventually coaxed down from the tank to take a walking tour of the camp with me as their guide. I talked in my English and they in theirs, and as we walked we were accompanied by a mass of prisoners. The prisoners applauded and crowded around to touch and pat the soldiers: a sacred moment for them, probably a frightening one for the soldiers. Even I was slapped on the back by my fellow-prisoners. A moment of high honor for me.

I took them first to tour the kitchen where the cooks

offered the soldiers some soup as a hospitable gesture. Looking into the proffered bowls, they tried to refuse. Oh, you cannot refuse their offering. They will be insulted, I managed to convey with frantic words and gestures. And so they each accepted a bowl, tasted a spoonful, complimented the cooks, and offered me their portions. I made short work of those two windfall bowls of watery mush, knowing the cooks could do nothing about my supreme feat of *Organisierung*, which was what we prisoners called the art of scrounging whatever we could for personal survival. The cooks and I showed them the extent of our small food stores, aging soup staples, coarse bread, and such.

We toured the barracks, the streets of the camp, the hospital jammed with the seriously ill, the crematorium which had stood cold since the flight of the SS a couple of days before. The Americans looked at the sea of emaciated prisoners, noted the appalling conditions under which they were clinging to existence, and from time to time as they walked, they had to step gingerly among torn-up parts of bodies lying around the camp grounds. These combat veterans returned to their tank looking almost sick from what they had seen.

The radio had reported back, while we were gone, that transportation was on the way to take the English-speaking one to headquarters in the town below. Soon a small, open vehicle arrived—like the one that followed the tanks into the camp—and I was driven out of the gates and down the road. A "jeep", the driver instructed me when I asked, and I squirreled away my new word. On the lower road as houses came into view I noticed white flags, sheets really, hanging from many windows. There was not a swastika in sight as we entered the town.

We pulled up at an inn that had been commandeered earlier in the day as company headquarters for the "F" Company, 3rd Cavalry Group, Mechanized. It was late afternoon. I was invited to wait in an outdoor *Biergarten*, and from there I watched a house across the street being forcibly vacated by the Americans. Three people were leaving with their small parcels of belongings. Later I heard that the house had belonged to an Austrian doctor and his family.

No one else came out of the houses of the town and nobody seemed even to peer from the windows. I turned my attention to two enormous tanks unattended on the streets outside the inn. Sherman tanks, I would soon be instructed, the same as the ones that liberated us. I stared in awe at the size of these machines; and as I did so, another jeep arrived with four more former prisoners. The five of us were escorted to the house across the street that the Americans had just "liberated" from an Austrian family. We were assigned the second floor as our quarters.

Addressing me in English, a soldier directed me to tell my new roommates that we were to clean ourselves up in the bathroom and help ourselves to any suitable clothes we could find in the closets. Several soldiers staggered in under the weight of five enormous cartons, which, I was told, were food rations for each of us to eat as we saw fit. We could hardly believe the size of the cartons, and no sooner had the door closed behind us than each of us tackled his carton with frantic intensity. To our bafflement we could not open them because they were bound in tight metal straps. We searched the house for a hammer, screwdriver, or cutters, and managed to find some tools. Taking turns, helping one another, expending a great deal of sweat and effort—for we were weak—we pried the boxes open and rifled in amazement through the contents. Each carton contained twenty army regulation meals for field use, plus candy bars, cigarettes, soap, and so on. We sat on the floor and started opening cans. We ate a bite of this, a bite of that, then opened more cans, anxious to taste each new offering. We ate candy, lit cigarettes, fondled the smooth soap, almost eating that as well. The floor was strewn with our food. Yet each of us was so protective of his own rations that we lunged at one another threateningly as one tried to taste from another's allotment, even though we all had the same rations. But as we filled up, we began to bargain and trade with one another over food preferences.

At long last we were sated and could turn our attention to the pleasures of a hot bath, though once again, not without haggling. We haggled over turns, over time in the bathtub, over supply of hot water.

"You've used enough hot water."

"I've hardly had time to soak compared with you. Let me bathe."

"I'm next after he's finished. Wait your turn!"

My turn came. I took up my wonderful soap and filled the bathtub with hot water. I scrubbed, soaked, and scrubbed again, but soon discovered, as each of us did, that there was no scrubbing off in one bathing session the ingrained dirt of years in the camps. My bathwater turned black, and when I crawled out to try the luxury of drying myself with a bath towel, I found I was still dirty. The evidence came off on the towel. I was to find that it would take me about two weeks of daily bathing to rid myself of the grime that had penetrated the pores of my body.

I looked at myself in a full-length mirror for the first time in years. Long accustomed to the emaciated appearance of my fellow prisoners, I was still surprised to see myself as skin over bone, a walking anatomy lesson. My cheeks were fallen in. My eyes had receded into my head. My skull was crudely shaven except for that stripe. I probably weighed about 85 pounds, an adult male, five feet and a half tall, almost 21 years old.

We rummaged through the closets and tried on clothing. Everything hung like sacks from our bodies. We looked comical but had not quite relearned the knack of laughing at ourselves. We made do, tied or belted ourselves in the middle, and flapped about like dressed-up birds.

Our stomachs full, our bodies cleaner and dressed in fresh clothing, we turned to one another for the first time as interested human beings. Who were we? One was a former high-ranking official of the Hungarian government. Another was of some former prominence no longer recalled. Two were mere boys, Jewish, the younger one no more than 10 or 11 years in age. I was a Sephardic Jew, a former diamond polisher from Amsterdam, Holland, who could speak a little English. We do not have much small talk to exchange. We are very tired. We have overeaten. We head for the beds and couches. I am tense. I am no longer in camp, as of this very day, and slowly becoming aware of it. No more regimentation. What am I supposed to do? What about tomorrow? How will I get by? Freedom is a worrisome state. I lie in a comfortable bed with a pillow and blankets, no longer stabbed by straw penetrating rough sacking, no longer scratching and pinching at lice. I mull things over uneasily. Sleep finally comes.

In the morning we returned to our food packages as to our new toys, and then to the bathtub for another good scrub. By mid-morning a couple of soldiers walked up our stairs.

"Which one of you speaks English?" one asked.

"I do."

"You're needed over at headquarters. Can you come with us now?"

I followed them back across the street to the inn. There the Americans needed help in interrogating a German, and I quickly found myself concentrating on the effort of translating from German to English. In spite of my limited ability, I made some sense with the translations, apparently, because I was asked to wait in order to be introduced to the officers. Once more I sat in the *Biergarten*; and while I waited, a number of soldiers gathered around to stare at me.

I stared at them too. Big boys they were, and very young looking for conquerors. Eventually, we looked away from one another, and I turned my attention to my surroundings. The *Biergarten* was a pleasant place, as romantic as a scene from an Austrian operetta. Soldiers sat at wooden tables in a flower-filled patio garden. Vine-covered trellises surrounded us. I was aware that I sat among my liberators as a free man in the village of Ebensee, that just yesterday I was locked in the concentration camp in the hills above. I looked down the short main street to a clear, blue, long lake, the end of which disappeared from sight among sharply-rising green mountains.

In my mind's eye I saw the forced march of hundreds of us ragged prisoners many weeks before as we struggled along the lakeside road, staggering, pulling along our stragglers, lest they be shot, through the main street of this village, over the bridge that crosses the river, and up that final hellish mountain road to the camp above, where we were thrown among thousands more gaunt prisoners who looked worse than we did. To shouted orders we assembled for the inevitable count on the big prison square. Oh, so tired we were, and even more thirsty, beyond hunger almost. We thought we were at the end of our endurance. Yet we were inwardly triumphant. We had all known for months that the end of the war was near, that we were being force-marched to interior worksites where our labor was desperately needed for Germany's failing war machine. We had pulled and dragged our weaker comrades along, determined that they not meet Nazi bullets with the end so near. For all of us who had been shoved out of the barges at Linz, and had walked some seventy-five kilometers to Ebensee, this was our great triumph over the Nazis, that we had brought every one of us in (though bitterly enough, many were to die during the harsh last weeks of our imprisonment in Ebensee).

I had not known until this moment that Ebensee was a pretty Austrian village, that the lake was refreshing to look upon, that the mountains were beautiful.

Anxiety filled me as a soldier stepped out to call me inside the inn. I was introduced to the officers in charge, a captain who was the company commander, and his lieutenants. They too were young, some perhaps younger than I. They explained to me that Germany had formally surrendered early that morning, that they were now assigned to pitch camp and help govern the area. They had been disturbed to discover that the territory they had captured and now controlled included the concentration camp they had opened the day before, freeing about 16,000 prisoners, for whom their small tank unit had no food or medical supplies. They asked me to serve with them as their interpreter in exchange for their care, since none of them spoke German. They needed information about the nature and problems of the prison population. They needed a go-between in order to communicate with prisoners.

This small contingent of the American military did indeed have a problem on their hands because most liberated prisoners were too weak or sick to walk away from the prison, and needed a great deal of help. Then there was the reality that most of them, like myself, were Jews who had no place to go if they did walk away. In the countries Germany overran, Jewish families had been systematically consigned to death camps, if not murdered on the spot, and their properties confiscated. On a smaller scale, other "inferior" peoples and individual enemies of the state had been thrown into these camps as well to be exterminated or to work until they rotted. We homeless survivors of the camps were called "displaced persons", the "D.P.'s", and at war's end all was confusion about what to do with us.

I jumped at the chance to stay on with my liberators as their interpreter. I was free all right, but freer than I had ever wanted to be, like a rudderless boat. Amsterdam had been home, but how could it be home now? My sister and parents had been taken away before me, and most of my relatives, friends, and neighbors. I was well aware that most of the Jews rounded up and sent to the camps had died there. Who would be left to hold out their arms to me in my old neighborhood? My dread was too great to want to find out.

I would be pleased to stay and serve as their interpreter, I told the American tank commander; but I had been so embarrassed by the many curious stares in my direction that in the next breath I asked him if the Americans could provide me with any clothing that fit.

A call went out immediately to some of the smaller soldiers in the outfit for any pants, shirts, underwear, socks, and shoes they could spare for my use. Within an hour I found myself transformed into a GI, which my clothing suppliers taught me was their term for themselves as common American servicemen. General Issue! A starving prisoner on Sunday, a regular GI on Monday, except for that damned stripe down my head, which a mirror appraisal of my new self seemed to emphasize. I walked across the street to the barber shop below the house in which I was billeted.

"Trim my hair down evenly," I ordered in German.

Seeing my head, the barber knew very well I was a former prisoner, though dressed as a GI, but he said nothing and I paid him nothing when he finished with his work.

With my help the officers interviewed my billet companions about what they had been through and where their homes were. Concerned about our starved bodies, they made arrangements for us to start taking three meals a day with the troops. We ate sumptuously, as if each meal were to be our last, and almost immediately the sudden switch to a rich and plentiful diet had a disastrous effect upon the five of us. We developed severe and chronic diarrhea. The officers then gave us permission to obtain food from the kitchen any time we felt hungry, but the diarrhea persisted. It took weeks for my intestines to be able to adjust to the new diet and for my body to function normally again.

Meanwhile, except to sleep, my home became the headquarters inn and particularly the pleasant *Biergarten* where I sat at my interviewing duties much of the day. Daily my English began to improve as I became better acquainted with my American liberators. I accumulated new words like possessions. I understood more. I expressed myself in more detail. In a few weeks I began to think in English as well as in German, and I took satisfaction in becoming more valuable in my work with each passing day.

The officers and men wanted to know all I could tell them about the camp in the hills above. They needed the information officially in order to obtain policy directives from higher up and to expedite the services of the United Nations Relief and Rehabilitation Administration (UN-

RRA), which had already been established to aid liberated populations in war-devastated areas. They were also personally curious about the unspeakable secrets of the Nazi regime that prisoners like ourselves were able to reveal: brutal torture, starvation, slave labor under unimaginable conditions. That was the good news—some of us were still alive! Death for millions of men, women, and children for racist and political reasons. That was the bad news. Some of the soldiers told of things they had witnessed or stories they had heard about appalling discoveries coming to light each day. We were numb with shock and could hardly comprehend the reality of the news we were exchanging with one another.

I told the men about the forced march of hundreds of us from Linz to Ebensee, that I had come there after stops at camps in Melk and Mauthausen, that I had been in one of the last transports out of Auschwitz as the Russians closed in. I told the Americans about our daily lives as prisoners in the Ebensee camp.

Ebensee camp was on a wide plateau in the mountains, whether natural or cut by man I did not know. One fence-surrounded ledge overlooked the valley. From there we could see the river and the road below, which led to Ebensee village to the right and the town of Bad Ischl to the left. The camp was entirely surrounded by an electric fence, which began and ended at a high arched gate at the entrance.

Streets of wooden prison barracks stood to one side of the assembly square, referred to in German as the *Appellplatz,* and the prison fence defined the limits of the square on the other side. An outside road ran alongside the fence, on the other side of which stood the barracks of our SS guards. Each of the prison barracks held about a thousand prisoners, who slept in narrow rows of bunks stacked one on top of another four tiers high. Within the fence and behind our barracks was the hospital and crematorium, both of which were always busy. The camp kitchen was also within the prison compound, recessed in an area beside the main gate.

Every morning we were awakened around 4 or 4:30 AM,

and lined up to receive a cup of hot liquid which tasted strange, but which was called tea. At least the brew was hot for it was the extent of our breakfast. We turned out on the *Appellplatz* for the countdown, then were sent out the gates on our daily march down the road passing the SS barracks on our way to the worksite. Our march was actually the slow shuffle of spent men, and we stumbled in our wooden clogs over cobblestones and rough places. When we reached the valley we turned up another mountain road, climbing laboriously upward until we reached an opening which led into a factory complex dug into the side of the mountain. The underground factory was a beehive of busy German workers and technicians. What they were producing there, we prisoners were not invited to understand nor were we in good enough physical shape to take much interest. We fetched and carried, stooped and lifted, hauled and pushed, did anything we were told as well as we were able. I did not care what was going on there. I concentrated on being able to make it down the mountain road and then up the torturous hill again to camp at the end of the day, where I could receive my hunk of bread and lie down. Down that hill, up that hill, week in, week out, we stumbled, and always the SS and the *Kapos* controlled us with their truncheons, shouting, "Los! Los! Mach schnell! Mach schnell!" Their rubber truncheons hit our backs regularly, but could not hasten us. With time we could no longer feel them, nor could we any longer hear the shouts of our tormentors.

The road grew steeper as we grew weaker. My memory of what the days were like is hazy. Like the others, I was severely affected by malnutrition. Without food the memory fades and awareness very much lessens. The will is reduced. In addition to the cup of "morning tea", we received a bowl of thin soup at midday on the work site, then in the evening a hunk of bread with a piece of margarine. In the factory we sometimes begged food from the Austrians we worked under, but we were ignored. At night sleep on a hard and lumpy bunk was our only luxury. We lately arrived Ebensee prisoners slept two to a bunk, and some unfortunates who arrived even later slept three to a bunk. To recall our sleep time as a luxury is to recall the depth of our misery.

I wanted the Americans to know about the exaltation in the camp when they liberated us. I wanted them to understand what it meant to me who had come through so much for so long. I told them of how the camp had been swept by rumors that the SS were going to machine-gun us because the war was near an end, and of how we whispered at night about how we might be able to resist. Those of us who were able and still had a will to survive, began to gather up club-like objects and to sharpen tools secretly with which we could either attack or defend ourselves. We did not know how many hours, or days, or weeks stretched before us until liberation, but survival became all-important.

One morning we awoke to realize that, by God, no bells had sounded to rouse us. The feeble lights were not on. The usual cries of "Aufstehen! Aufstehen!" "Los! Los!" "Heraus! Heraus!" were not heard. No one called us out for the morning count, or lined us up to go to work. There was no hot tea. An oppressive silence hung over the camp. Our routine was upset. Fear crept into our barracks. What was next for us?

Slowly, noise arose in the camp. The sound grew. There was excitement outside. We rushed out to join people running around the streets between barracks, shouting the unbelievable news:

"They've gone! They've gone! The SS have left. They've sneaked off in the night."

"We have the camp to ourselves except for a couple of old *Volkswehr* at the gate!"

We were slow to believe it. We thought it could not be true. We rushed to the fence, the fence that overlooked the road and the Nazi barracks. And right! They were gone. No smoke came from the chimneys of their housing. Their wagons were gone. Someone discovered that the electricity in the fence had been turned off, and we pushed against it, cheering. But the fence was strong and we were weak. Two old *Volkswehr* with rifles on their shoulders stood guard outside the gate, two old men to guard thousands of us. They bargained with us, asking us not to try to attack them because they were only obeying orders and acting as our caretakers until our liberators arrived. For our part we were all too weak and apprehensive to think of doing anything other than agreeing with the old men that we would await liberation.

But we could have used some hot tea. No food was being prepared from whatever small stores had been left us. Camp organization had shut down. Still we rejoiced that we did not have to go down that damned hill anymore. We did not have to enter those shafts to labor within the mountain.

Almost immediately the *Blockälteste* and the *Kapos* organized to run the camp. They inventoried supplies and issued orders to the kitchen for the serving of meals. Already severely underfed, we now were further rationed because the camp leaders realized they should stretch our stores as far as possible, not knowing when liberation would come. Many among us were so close to death that they did not care any more. The leaders passed orders that those who gave up caring for their own health would be punished by their fellow prisoners. The only work we had to do now was to clean our barracks and to take care of the sick. There was no saving those who were on the way out, but keeping life in those who could be saved became very important. Tension built up, and yet at the same time there was a mood of jubilation in the camp. We've done it! We're out of it! We cannot afford to die now! (And still, some persisted in dying.)

Yet we were underfed, starving. Nursed grievances flared, and suddenly deadly revenge parties raged through the camp. Some of the prisoners were singled out for attack. These were men who had reputations as tough *Kapos,* unfeeling *Blockälteste,* informers. Weak prisoners managed to attack and kill these men, then literally tear their bodies apart. Now we accustomed ourselves to detouring around a head, a leg, a limbless torso—pieces of human flesh and bone lying around the grounds of our camp. Incredible vengeance had had its day. But for many of us who had lived with death in the camps, this scene was not surprising. How cool we were: "He had it coming, the son of a bitch!"

There was a miraculous happening too, and unforgettable. Flags began to appear on the fence overlooking the valley. One by one they began to appear along the fence until there were quite a few of them. Great flags, not miniatures. I had not been aware of my fellow prisoners making or stealing these flags, nor did I know from what they could have made them or how they could have hidden them. But they appeared: the French flag, the Polish flag, the Dutch flag, the Hungarian flag, the Belgian flag, and there were others. I pictured how it must have looked from the valley road, a ribbon of festive flags on the shelf of our mountain. I was light-headed, delighted with the flags, already feeling free. I was fairly bursting with hope and good will. We did not have to work anymore or live in fear of anyone or even take our caps off to anyone. The old guards at the gate were dress-ups, and more than likely had no bullets in their rifles.

We waited. It may have been a couple of days after the disappearance of the SS that a shout arose from the watchers at the fence in the early morning. "There they are! There they are!"

Everyone rushed to look. Fighting for a place at the fence myself, I saw trucks moving eastward, toward Ebensee village. That was significant. If they were traveling from west to east, they were not retreating; they were coming in. Several hours passed. Gradually, we heard a rumbling on the road we used to walk up and down every morning and evening. It was a noise we had not heard before. Like dammed up water suddenly rushing loose, the prisoners flowed toward the fence near the road to watch and listen to the sound growing louder.

I tried to describe to the Americans about the miracle of how it felt from inside the prison to see their great tanks pull up outside our gate and to see the rifle of the *Volkswehr* being broken over the turret and hung over the gate to our camp.

II

During the first days of liberation, the Americans got busy on their radio, transmitting and receiving messages about supplies that were desperately needed. For our small unit, of which I was now a part, these days brought enormous problems, most of them pertaining to my erstwhile fellow prisoners. I would wake up unbelieving of my good luck to be no longer among those sorry men, no longer hungry, not having to learn what it was like to be homeless and rootless. My liberating tank outfit had given me a home, food, companionship, and a job engaging my mind instead of physical labor. I had clean, warm clothing, a daily bath, and a real bed to sleep in under wool blankets. I did not look down the road or think about tomorrow. I clung to my rescuers.

The prisoners continued to live in the squalid camp above, waiting, trying to gather strength, looking forward to the arrival of UNRRA relief. Left to their own devices, they cooperated to maintain the camp themselves. Food rations gradually improved but nutrition was still far from adequate, and many prisoners continued to fail and die. The American company commander made a trip up to the camp to assess the situation. Bodies were accumulating at a hazardous rate. Down in the town the Americans confronted the townspeople, with me along as interpreter, about permitting such an inhuman camp to operate in their midst. "Oh, we had no idea what was going on up there," they protested. "We were not consulted. We did not see it. How could we know?"

"That's a lot of shit," I blurted angrily in German. "Did we not march by the thousands through your town and up that road to the camp? How many of you showed sympathy or tried to help? Did we not work six days a week in that mountain factory side by side with you townspeople? How many of you shared your food with us? Did you not see and smell the stench and smoke that floated down from the camp every day? What did you think was happening?"

The Americans ordered all townspeople, young and old, adults and children, to march up to the camp and through it, then to help one another carry the bodies for burial. The townspeople rebelled at this odious order, but in the end they had no choice. All of them filed reluctantly up to the camp, a sobering experience. As they brought down the emaciated, stinking bodies, people fainted, vomited, or cried hysterically. The Austrians all felt that the Americans had imposed an unspeakable indignity upon them, but they did as told. The bodies were buried alongside the road leading to Bad Ischl.

As the prisoners grew stronger, they began to venture down the hill during the day in increasing numbers. They promenaded up and down the short main street which extended from the nearby lakeshore to about two blocks beyond the inn. Many foraged through the town and countryside, scavenging for food, plundering whatever they could. They derided any local citizen who had the guts to come out of his house. The five of us privileged prisoners, while taking our lunch and dinner with the troops in the sunlit *Biergarten,* would experience the awkward shame of feeling the stare of our fellow prisoners on our plates as we ate. We tried not to look, but if there were men there we knew, we took some food over for them to eat. Yet the company kitchen could not feed them all. The officers and GI's lavished care and attention on the few of us—we were symbolic of what they had fought for. The rest were too many and they had to wait for the establishment of supply lines.

Acting as an interpreter between my fellow prisoners and the American authorities became my most important job. All grievances and petitions were transacted through me as I sat day after day in the *Biergarten*. Prisoners were brought in on complaints of the local citizens for stealing, or for this infringement or that. The GI's were reluctant to discipline them except superficially because their sympathies lay with the prisoners. Nevertheless, some semblance of order was gradually established.

I was sitting one day at my duties when a loud tumult was heard. A great crowd surged toward the *Biergarten*. The prisoners were dragging in a man they had captured, one of the former SS guards at the camp. The prisoners demanded immediate justice, preferably theirs. The officers posed questions in English which I interpreted into German for the SS man, then back to English. The prisoners stood outside the *Biergarten* heckling and shouting for the GI's to turn the SS guard over to them. The officers refused because the captured man had to be considered a prisoner of war. They called Military Government for instructions and were told to escort the man to headquarters in a nearby town; but the whole street was filled with threatening prisoners, making the Americans extremely nervous. The officers decided to relieve the situation by allowing some "fun" with the prisoner. One of the GI's had an armband with a swastika on it. This he pulled up on the SS man's arm and made him raise it while saluting Nazi-style, "Heil Hitler!" "Heil Hitler!" Everyone derided him loudly and mercilessly. He was made to march up and down the *Biergarten* in goosestep, still saluting. "Heil Hitler!"

The GI's snapped pictures of him. Our carryings-on may have resembled a Punch and Judy show, but we felt a need to go through with this. Again, as their symbol, perhaps, I was invited by the GI's to take the SS guard into a back room and punch him at will. I knew damn well I was too weak, and even still afraid of him. I declined the honor. Eventually the officers ordered the captured Nazi driven off to military headquarters.

Not much more than a week passed before UNRRA personnel and supplies arrived, bringing to Ebensee an extensive aid program. For those who had waited, the time had seemed long, but the medical, feeding, and rehabilitation programs quickly transformed the concentration camp into a supervised hospital and way station. By then I had gained bodily strength. I was becoming more self-assured. With UNRRA personnel assisting the prisoners at the camp site, my interpreting duties became much lighter. "Can you drive an automobile, Max?" a GI asked. I laughed. In Holland almost everyone rode bicycles. "Of course, I can't drive. I've only ridden as a passenger in trucks and your jeeps once in awhile."

"Well, that won't do, Max. Everyone in this unit can drive every piece of equipment we've got. If you're going to stay with us, hell, you've at least got to know how to drive a jeep."

To my delight some American soldiers took me out on mountainous Austrian roads and began to teach me to drive, a crash course in every respect. This is the steering wheel. This is the accelerator. This is the brake. This is how you clutch, shift gears, go forward or in reverse. My adventures in the jeep with my GI teachers were both hair-raising and hilarious, exhilarating and frightening. Finally, within a few days, I was allowed to take the thing out by myself. I could drive a jeep.

The Americans turned their attention to teaching me to shoot. Again, a necessity, they told me, if I was to stay with their combat outfit. In part, there was concern for our protection as roving bands of prisoners became bolder and a few of them, menacing. Part, too, was the fun of fraternizing military style with an admiring liberated prisoner from the "old country." These American boys, most of them younger than I, enjoyed teaching me to shoot rifles, revolvers, forty-fives, and after a few weeks, even burp guns. Heady stuff for a tough, young survivor who had never held such weapons before.

Word reached the camp one day that General Patton, Commander of the 3rd Army, was due to come through on an inspection trip. The whole company bustled about, polishing, refurbishing, reshaping themselves into correct military order. A grand villa outside of town was chosen in which to install their distinguished leader. Along with the cooks, I was delegated to go out to the villa to interpret between the local help and the Americans.

At a huge victory dinner thrown in his honor, I was able to see Patton. He was a tall man, a huge man in riding boots and breeches. He wore two conspicuous revolvers at his hips. Even without the military trappings and hardware he would have dominated the room with his booming voice and imposing personality. The Americans had long since briefed me on the progress of the war from the Allies' point of view, and on the bloody battles and eventual triumphs of the 3rd Army in particular. I was awed to be in the presence of General Patton. To me he was an American hero.

I had no desire or reason to return to the concentration camp on the hill until several weeks after my liberation, and then only once when I had to present myself to UNRRA officials in order to obtain documented discharge papers. Without this documentation I was in danger of being picked up for the growing D. P. camps because I had no official status with the American Army. I was allowed to drive the jeep up there myself, cocky and in American uniform, in the company of a couple of GI friends. At first the officials tried to dismiss me as a GI playing games. Abandoning my initial bravado I began to explain my circumstances in earnest. In the end, I received a small document confirming that the number on my left forearm, 139829, was that of an Auschwitz prisoner, that I had also been held in camps at Mauthausen, Melk, and Ebensee, and that I had been liberated from the latter on the 6th of May, 1945.

At some time during the course of my service with the tank unit, I was asked by some officials if I would be interested in joining a large contingent of prisoners who were awaiting release to Palestine where they planned to help pioneer a new Jewish state. I told them no, thanks, that I had never been devout, that I did not wish to live in a nation composed only of Jews, that I had never lived that way before, except in the camps.

My 20-year-old mind had already rejected a return to Holland. I could not yet deal with what had happened to my family and to me there after the occupation. I knew there was no one close for me to return to, and I saw no other reason to return. I had lived through years of degradation and dehumanization as a Jew, first in occupied Holland, then in the camps. I wanted to turn from the stigma of it, start all over in a new country as an individual, not as a Jew. I was not ready to look to the future. I clung anxiously to the tank outfit that had adopted me, to their open friendliness and encouragement. I felt safe so long as I stayed among them.

III

One by one the former prisoners with whom I bunked disappeared as headquarters command took charge of their repatriation or resettlement. Within a few weeks I was assigned to housing with the GI's. I pulled routine duty with them and accompanied them on patrols. I was their devoted volunteer "recruit." So it was to my total surprise to be called to the command office one morning and told, "Max, we're moving out. We've been ordered down to Trieste, but, unfortunately, you're not going to be able to come along."

"Sir," said I, "this is my outfit. I can serve down there just as well..."

"Max, we have been glad to have you with us, and you have served well, but we cannot take you along. We may see some action in Trieste, and after we get that ruckus wound up we're scheduled to go home. Why don't you go home too, Max? You've got to face going back to Holland sometime. Why not now?"

My world was coming apart again, but there was no pleading my case. The "ruckus" referred to was an impasse over the disposition of Trieste between Marshall Tito of Yugoslavia and the Italians. The 3rd Cavalry Tank Regiment had been ordered to Trieste to hold Tito in check. Even if the unit did see action, I was more frightened at the idea of being left behind, and made up my mind that I would not settle for it.

By the morning of departure I had persuaded some of the boys with whom I was close to allow me to climb into their tank and sit at the bottom. The tank convoy moved off and I was with them. We rode southward all day, pulling in for bivouac late in the afternoon. Everybody fell out to stretch and relax, including me. We were lined up for a head count, and there I was. My strategy had been to rely on their letting me stay once they saw my determination to get this far. But, alas, the first sergeant walked over to me:

"Max, what'n hell are you doing here? I've got strict orders. You can't come with us. You've got to go back, as we've told you before. I know how you feel, but it's out of our hands."

I burst into tears. I had truly looked upon the tank unit as my new home, my friends of whom I was part. The boys with whom I had lived and pulled duty all stood around me and commiserated. They tried to argue with the sergeant, and when the officers saw a budding conspiracy they called me over and repeated what the sergeant had told me before. I was not a member of the U.S. Army and I could not accompany them. They advised me to return to Ebensee, report to the authorities, and then start back for Amsterdam. They assigned an officer to drive me back to Radstadt, the nearest seat of Military Government. He was to explain to authorities there who I was, where I came from, and where I was to go. A lieutenant drove me to Radstadt that same evening. As ordered, he explained my circumstances to the authorities there. My papers were scrutinized, and I was assigned a bunk for the night. In the morning I was driven back to the highway and permitted to hitchhike toward Ebensee.

Two GI's in a jeep picked me up, assuming I was one of them. I did not deny it. When they heard my accent and some faulty answers to their questions about the States, they became suspicious and wanted to see my dogtags.

I had none to show them, of course, but I showed them my papers and tried to explain my story. The doubt in their minds had not been erased when we arrived at a roadblock at the village of Aich-Assach. The GI's were waved on but I was detained because I was in American uniform, but without dogtags. My accent, uniform, and story made me highly suspect, it seemed.

I was ushered to a bench along the outside wall of the Command Post building to await questioning. An officer came out and heard my story. He was patient. Another officer joined him in questioning me. They gave me a cigarette.

As we talked some Austrians approached the American officers and began addressing them in German. Not understanding a word that was said, the officers called over a member of their Intelligence and Reconnaissance unit. This soldier struggled to understand and translate, but much of what the Austrians were trying to say was lost. I could not resist putting my recent training to use and clarifying the dialogue all around. The group began to turn to me for interpretation, and within short order the Austrians' problem was understood and resolved. The Austrians left, and the Americans walked back inside the Command Post.

After some minutes one of the officers came back outside, thanked me for my translating services, and introduced himself. He was Lieutenant Colonel Arthur H. Clark, commander of the First Battalion, 319th Infantry Regiment Headquarters Company, 80th Infantry Division. He directed me to accompany him inside and to explain once again to other officers my background and events that had brought me to the village of Aich-Assach. I was asked to leave, then after sitting outside awhile longer, called back inside. Colonel Clark acknowledged that after checking out my papers and noting my concentration camp number on my left forearm, they believed my story. It was mentioned that they were currently on the alert for some former SS Corps members who were rumored to be hiding in the mountains hereabout, which was their reason for checking me out so carefully. They had been impressed with the help I had just given them in translating, and asked me, in view of my separation from "F" Company, 3rd Cavalry, because of reassignment, if I would serve in a similar capacity with the First Battalion, 319th Infantry Regiment.

Would I serve? I was elated, but at the same time a cautious thought passed through my mind.

"Sir," I said, "I would very much like to serve as your interpreter, but there is one condition that you will have to agree to before I accept."

"Ohhhh?" questioned the colonel.

"If and when you get reassigned, you must take me with you."

"Mr. Garcia, we cannot take you back to the States with us. You must get that straight."

"I know that, sir. I am asking that while the 319th is in Europe that I stay assigned to it wherever you go."

Again the officers asked me to leave so they could discuss this condition. I was amazed at my boldness for I desperately wanted to stay. Here was I summoning the nerve to make a contract with another party. If they wanted something from me, I must have something in return. Had I not just learned one more time the bitter fact that I was quite expendable? I was worth no more than my services, so I had to gamble that the value of my services could be transformed into some security for me. I was soon relieved to hear the colonel's affirmative answer. "Okay, Mr. Garcia, we're going to try it your way, that is if you behave and do the best you can for us. We can't guarantee that we'll be able to take you with us if we are reassigned, but if you keep your end of the bargain, we promise to try."

We shook hands. I was introduced to the officer with Colonel Clark, Captain Jesse R. Miles. He, in turn, introduced me to a sergeant in charge of the Intelligence and Reconnaissance unit to which I was to be assigned. Scheduled into the routines of my new platoon, I now wore the 80th Division patch on my left sleeve and the blue braid of an infantryman's cap. In addition to regular hours of rotating duty at the Command Post, I was sent for whenever a real problem in communication arose. I was housed with the I. and R. men in a nearby farmhouse, and took my meals with the troops. A little scrip money from the Soldiers Fund was given me to buy cigarettes and a few necessities at the PX. The men exchanged news from their hometowns and their girlfriends, but mostly they talked about baseball and baseball players, a summertime subject that seemed to bring all Americans close together. I learned the names of major league teams and their star players, and tried to talk about baseball too.

Awakening one morning with a headache and fever, I went on sick call. The doctor sent me for examination to the field hospital, which was in a town some distance away. I was examined, given rest and medication, then discharged within a few days. The doctors had questioned me as they read my record, since I had no military documentation, but in the end they discharged me as routinely as any GI, with no strings attached. I hitchhiked rides by military ambulances back to Aich-Assach, by way of Gmunden, and was congratulated by Captain Miles upon my return. He had not expected to see his interpreter again as he had assumed I would be identified in the hospital as a D. P. and sent off to a D. P. center for processing.

I went back to duty. Our town was nestled in breathtaking Alpine country, but this was very high terrain for a "lowlander." I developed headaches which intensified with my growing anxiety over rumors that the 319th was about to be reassigned. I inquired directly, and Captain Miles confirmed that the 319th was getting ready to move to Bavaria. Most troops would be going by train. A few would travel by truck with the supplies.

"Remember our deal, Captain, about bringing me along? Am I on your list to move?"

"Max, I'm too busy to think about that right now. Let's take it up later."

He never did. Moving day came. Most of the men

were loaded onto trucks and sent to the train station. I was all packed up like everyone else, but without orders. This time I had a whole duffel bag full of personal belongings, and was sitting on it, hoping for orders, when Captain Miles drove up in a jeep.

"C'mon, Max, let's go."

I hopped in fast, throwing my duffel bag in the back seat. "You're taking me with you, Captain?"

"That's our deal, isn't it, Max? When we can control it, you can come along with us. We're going to lead the convoy. Colonel Clark wanted you to ride with me in case we need your interpreting help along the way."

I sank into the seat, relieved and grateful, for they had not let me down. As the point vehicle of a large convoy of trucks and staff cars, we drove north through Salzburg, then west into Bavaria and to our destination, Bad Wörishofen. We were still in mountain country, but no longer so high. The headaches let up.

Our convoy arrived on a tree-lined street of the prosperous-looking resort town of Bad Wörishofen. The Americans knew that the place had served as a resort for the Nazis during the war, and so had been little altered through those years. The town presented itself, therefore, as an ideal post for battle-weary American occupying forces.

The 319th set about immediately to alter the town's satisfied appearance. I was ordered to enter all houses on the left hand side of the pretty street on which we had chosen to stop, and to demand that they be vacated within two hours. I took to my assignment with enthusiasm.

"Attention, occupants!" I would say, "You must clear your home for the use of the American occupying forces immediately. You have two hours in which to gather your personal belongings and get out. You must leave all furniture, beds, bed clothing, and kitchen utensils..."

"How can you do this?" they asked. "It is illegal!"

"You must allow us to see the Bürgermeister first."

"Go see him, but pack what you need first."

"Where is my family to go? We have no place to go."

"That's your problem, madam. I've no place to go either."

Oust them I did, and within the time suggested to me. The problems of resettlement were left to the families. Some of us from I. & R. were assigned that afternoon to a comfortable two-story house at the end of the street.

There was little of importance for us to do now, and the company was permitted to relax in Bad Wörishofen. Time slowed down. We tossed baseballs back and forth. Military vehicles parked everywhere. GI's in great numbers roamed the streets and through luxury hotels where they were currently billeted. Through the windows we looked at the elegant interiors of stores that had once flourished, but now were closed. We gathered evenings in beerhalls and listened to American dance music on records provided by the U.S.O.

I imitated the Americans and allowed the townspeople to mistake me for one of the occupying Americans. Headquarters eventually got wind of my deception and took me to task for it, ordering me, from then on, to wear identifying Dutch flag insignia. I looked around town to find someone who could stitch a flag patch for me in a neat and interesting way, and was directed to a sister in a convent, who consented to sew me a handsome Dutch flag. I, in turn, sewed the patch carefully, and with budding pride, on the pocket of my shirt.

My buddies and the officers of our unit, a few at a time, began to try to get through to me the importance of planning a future for myself beyond the 319th. Though they were familiar with my history, they urged me to go home and try to find some surviving relatives. I am sure they could see my loneliness in my desperation to cling to them. They wanted to help and to see me on my feet before they left, reminding me that I would be left behind when they were sent home within the next few months.

The officers gave me a leave of absence and permission to hitchhike home. I agreed to return to Amsterdam, longing to return yet profoundly reluctant to arrive there. I was too aware of what I would find. From the time I was 15 years old, [he became 16 in June, 1940] when Germany had invaded Holland in May, 1940, I had learned what it was to be isolated as a Jew, first from our fellow townspeople, then gradually from each other as the Nazis hounded and hunted us like criminals, thinning our numbers at will. I knew that almost everyone in my large family of relatives had been picked up before my hiding place was discovered, that my sister was gone, my parents were gone. I knew about the sealed freight cars in which we were all shipped off, and about the death camps at the other end of the ride.

Yet, here I was, alive, and asked by my new friends to go home and resume my life. Guilt and dread and fear engulfed me, but I reached out for the hope the boys spoke of. The Americans longed for home. Rips and tears would be mended at home. Home was home. The recorded hit songs of the mid-forties sang to us about the joys that awaited us at home. Everyone wanted to go home.

I hitchhiked home. It was before the atomic bomb fell on Hiroshima, sometime in early August, 1945, for I was in Amsterdam on V-J Day, August 15. I spent about a week in Amsterdam. What I did there comes back in puffs of remembrance, like my last hitched ride into town on the back of a Dutchman's motorcycle. He picked me up some distance outside of town and tore with me over gravel roads on the most frightening ride of my life. I could feel the wheel skipping beneath us, and held on with an iron grip. After all I had gotten through, I thought, what a way for me to go. The streets of Amsterdam were a welcome sight.

I walked the streets where I used to live. I walked through the old Jewish area on the other side of the Amstel River. It was a jumble of torn-up housing where blocks and blocks of ancient buildings had housed generations of families. I walked up and down the Amstellaan and some of our neighborhood canals. I went downtown. The "Mokummers," as Amsterdamers called themselves, bustled around me, everyone speaking Dutch. Because Holland had been liberated by the Canadian Army, Canadian soldiers swarmed through the streets, mingling with the Dutch. On V-J Day the cafes on the Rembrandtsplein and the Kalverstraat overflowed with townspeople and Canadians who were celebrating in a subdued mood the A-bomb-hastened victory over Japan that brought an end to World War II. Some Canadians invited me to have a drink with them, and I drank with my country's liberators, an uneasy stranger in my own town.

There is much that my mind refuses to recall. I do not know where I slept. I do not remember visiting the family who had hidden me during the Nazi occupation until someone had reported my hiding place. Yet I have pictures of the wedding of one of the sons immediately after the war, and I have my architecture books, the books I had left with that family when I was forced to flee. There is an added architectural volume inscribed to me from the newly-wedded son and his wife, Lou and Rita— no last name inscribed and the name of that family not remembered.

Some of my wanderings I do remember. I walked again into my old neighborhood and down Graaff Florisstraat where I had last lived. I approached the building my family had occupied, and looked over the tenants' names posted by their doorbells. An unknown name was posted for our flat, and, in fact, there was not one familiar name among the listed tenants.

I crossed the street to the walk-up flats opposite ours. Sure enough, one familiar name was posted still It belonged to a gentile family who had begun a friendship with my parents when my father sold them some cheese on the black market of wartime Amsterdam. Papa had told me when he had last visited me in hiding that he was planning to leave our personal papers and valuables with this family. I rang the bell and was admitted.

The couple registered shock and surprise when I identified myself, then hugged me and cried. Old griefs were remembered. I inquired about my family and other neighborhood Jews we knew in common. They told me they had not heard again from any of these people. The woman brought out a shoebox which she placed in my lap.

My tears fell in splotches on the familiar old papers, the wedding and birth certificates and other records. My mother and father at various stages and ages looked out from photographs. My sister, Sienie, and I were recorded in careful poses from birth to teenage. The smiling faces of my relatives looked at me once more, even my whole grammar school class under Mevrouw van der Roest. There was my mother's silver etched needle case, my father's brown leather cigar case and bone holder, my Bar Mitzvah watch that had been my grandfather's gift to me. My father's diamond stickpin and my mother's ring were not there. I asked about these items and was told that they had never been included in the box. Maybe, after all, my father had changed his mind about leaving such valuables behind. I did not need them. I had my family's records and photographs. From that time on, I toted them with me everywhere, looking at them only at times when I needed to remind myself that I once had belonged to a firmly rooted family. I thanked the couple with genuine gratitude for keeping my family's records through the occupation.

I walked to the house of a Dutch police officer with whom my father had worked closely in the black market during the occupation, and to whom I knew my father had entrusted a valuable stamp collection. He was shocked to see me, and, at first, denied that he had ever been given my father's stamps. We talked at some length and he capitulated, admitting that he had once held the stamps in his possession, but explaining that the reduced circumstances of his own family's lives had forced him to sell them. He told me how the occupied Dutch had been starved and bled white to feed the German war machine as the war progressed. He sold the stamps, he told me, after the Jews had all been rounded up and sent off, and after talk had gone around that all of them had been put to death. I asked him why the old buildings of the Jewish area had been gutted. He told me that during the severe winter of 1944-45, just passed, these empty buildings had been torn apart for their wood by townspeople who had no other fuel to heat their frigid homes.

I had seen my neighborhood and my town, but just as I had feared, there was no one there to greet me with joy and to encourage me to begin again. I thought of my confident American friends and the new kind of life they had shown me. My mind no longer wavered. I did not want to stay in Holland. I decided to return immediately to my unit in Bad Wörishofen.

I hitchhiked to Maastricht, a rest camp for GI's located on a train line into Germany. The Dutch border was controlled by the Allies to prevent the free passage of war criminals and various other unauthorized refugees. Only Allied military personnel could cross these borders unchallenged. I had been given a military pass into Holland, but no return pass. American M.P.'s controlled the Maastricht railroad station, which was the last border train stop before entering Germany. Dutch police patrolled the station as well. I noticed these police eying my Dutch flag insignia on an American uniform. Quickly, I approached the American M.P.'s for help, explaining that I was a Dutchman assigned as a translator to the 319th Infantry Regiment in Bad Worishöfen, that I had hitchhiked home for a week, had lost my pass, and wanted to return. The M.P.'s helped me to board the train without being questioned by the Dutch police. The train puffed off to Cologne. The kilometers clicked by and I was grateful for the distance that was lengthening between me and my homeland, glad to be fleeing before someone could grab me and make me stay.

From the train I took to the roads again until I was back on our company street. My ears and eyes were greeted with the familiar thwack and thump of a baseball being hurled from glove to glove.

"My God!" Will you look who's back?"

"Max! You ain't ever goin' t'leave us. What happened?"

"Well, I just can't stand it without you guys. Besides, no one is left for me to go home to."

Somebody got on the squawkbox with the news that Max was back. The street began to fill up with my American GI friends.

PART 2

A DUTCH JEWISH FAMILY OF DIAMOND WORKERS

Elie Rodriguez Garcia (Max's father), as a young man, left; Elie's sister Jaantje, middle; his brother Maurits, right. Date of photo unknown.

1924—1937

Dismissal time at Graaff Floris Primary school found Appie Klaverstyn, Robbie Bleekrode, and me dashing for the school yard to play soccer or kickball with our schoolmates. At the dinner hour we walked home together, for we lived in apartments on the same block. During our free time at home we played together on a brick-paved island, interspersed with trees, in the middle of Saffierstraat, on which our apartment fronted. Sometimes we trotted down to the Amstel River a block away to watch boat club members racing their shells of all sizes. In winter we skated on that same Amstel or on the canals. We strapped on our wooden skates and joined our friends on the ice, lunging forward with long strides, hands clasped behind our backs.

Appie, Robbie, and I had been born in Amsterdam within a day of one another in 1924, one on June 27, one on June 28, and one on the 29th. We went through most of the primary school years together and grew to know one another like brothers. (My parents named me Meyer at birth after my deceased grandfather, Meyer Veerman, but my family and friends always called me Max.)

Ours was a working class neighborhood of people employed, for the most part, in the diamond industry. We were mostly Jews. There were a few gentiles and mixed marriages, such as Appie Klaverstyn's parents, and, like Appie's father, there were those among us who did not work in the diamond industry.

My father was a diamond polisher, and highly skilled.

My grandfather, too, had spent a lifetime in the diamond industry, until his retirement. But during my lifetime my grandfather lived in Antwerp where he had moved after retirement to work as a *shamus* in a small synagogue there. He had also remarried since the early death of my grandmother, whom I had never known. It was evidence of my father's skill that he remained employed in the industry during the early 30's when the depression deepened and most of our neighbors were laid off.

Elias Rodriguez Garcia, my father, was a handsome man and well proportioned. There was a good-natured set to his face and an often seen twinkle in his eye that advertised a mischievious, bold, but cheerful disposition. No matter how bad times became, papa would strive to make the best of his situation and show an optimistic face to his family and the world. My father could be deprived of just about everything and still take a forward-looking viewpoint. He tried to find matters to laugh about when others were merely depressed at the ever-worsening problems of our lives. As a family, we warmed ourselves at the hearth of his good humor.

My father was also a political man, an ardent Social Democrat, and an active member of his labor union. For him the fight for "social democracy" was a crusade of the working man to introduce social reforms by democratic means. He and others of the movement were opposed to radical socialism, or worse, communism. These latter movements, they believed, spelled violence and repressive government. Social Democrats held that social reforms must stem from reason and gain acceptance gradually by democratic processes. They wanted public ownership of community service industries and basic heavy industries. Their socialism did not extend to the small businessman or farmer.

Papa looked on with alarm at the rapid expansion of fascism in Italy and Germany. He was incensed by rumors of purges and liquidations resulting from the Russian Communist system that emerged from their bloody revolution and civil war. Over the years his convictions strengthened that these systems should be opposed. I was taught that the fascists, believing in privilege for the few, state regimentation for the many, and the communists, believing in complete state control to create equal pay and goods for all, took off in opposite directions but traveled in a circle to meet at the same point. That point meant forceful compliance or death for the average man.

Pretty and amply-made Rosette Veerman Rodriguez Garcia, my mother, was easy-going and very much under the strong influence of father. Still, she voiced her anxieties more than my father, about us children, about the times; and she had her own close family to fall back upon for reassurance. Mother was the youngest daughter in a family of eight Veerman offspring, all of whom were married and living in Amsterdam. To my young eyes, her strengths were those of a devoted homemaker, wife, and mother. If a cake was needed for a special occasion among our large family of relatives, my mother was usually asked to bake it. That is, she put the ingredients together in her kitchen, a process my sister and I loved to watch, before taking the batter out to the baker for baking. Our kitchens had no ovens, no ice boxes, not even hot water, yet my mother cooked well. Her sisters dropped by often for recipes, and it was readily acknowledged that hers were the outstanding dishes at any family gathering. She made a particularly delicious *boterkoek* from a family recipe that I try to duplicate every year to this day. When sewing had to be done by anyone in the family, mother's advice was also sought. She sewed for all of us, and in lean years did "piece work" at home and in sewing ateliers.

There was much about my mother I did not know because as soon as I was old enough to walk to school by myself I was out of the house and playing in the streets. The occupations of my mother and sister hardly interested me.

On a trip back to Amsterdam a great many years later, I visited at length with the senior Klaverstyns. Mrs. Klaverstyn reminded me that she and my mother had worked in the same sewing atelier on the Jodenbreestraat, recuperated in the hospital together when Appie and I were born, and were close friends as young women. She remembered my mother's ready intelligence and how willingly she took on new duties with my father's changes in fortune. I was aware that both of my parents had a passion for opera and operetta, but I had not known that my mother went with her friends almost every week to enjoy the operettas at the Rembrandt Theatre. Mrs. Klaverstyn recalled that the "girls" were particularly fond of one singing star, Else Grassan, and that at one point they gathered their courage and sent her a note that they would like to meet her. The singer acknowledged the note and set a date to receive them. My mother and her friends chipped in to buy an elegant box of bonbons, only to suffer great disappointment at the interview because the singer stood chatting with them for only a few minutes, accepted their gift of bonbons, but did not offer so much as a cup of tea.

With another anecdote, Mrs. Klaverstyn told me of my mother's infatuation with elegant clothes and expensive hats, a taste she was hardly ever in a position to indulge. "One day she told the girls at the atelier she had seen a so wonderful little hat in the window of Van Sweeden, a hat shop in the Utrechtsestraat. Oh! like a poem! But so sorry she had not enough money yet; so she had to wait and save money, for she should have it! Well, one of her friends, Saar Slager, was a poet and that day the girls sang in an operetta melody the following song:

Het mooiste dat Rozet op aarde kan verlangen,
Is't hoedje dat ze by Van Sweeden heeft zien hangen,
Maar daar Rozetje nu dat hoedje nog niet kan betalen.
Kan zy dat hoedje by Van Sweeden nog niet halen!

The most beautiful thing on earth that Rozetje could desire,
Is a small hat she saw displayed in the window at Van Sweeden;
But because Rozetje cannot pay for that little hat,
She cannot pick up that hat at Van Sweeden.

My sister, Sippora, whom we called Sienie, was said to

have our Grandmother Garcia's good looks. By teenage she was well on her way to becoming a beautiful young woman. Though we shared a bedroom until she was picked up by the Nazis at the age of 16, I noticed little about her except that she liked sweets only too well. One and a half years younger than I, and a girl, I gave her little of my attention as we grew up together.

Our family orbited mainly within the circle of my mother's family, the Veermans, all of whom lived within easy distances. Though my Portuguese-descended father's relatives also lived near us in Amsterdam, my mother, Rozetje, as she was called, steered our relationships toward her own close family. My father, called Elie, was even looked upon as a bit crazy by the Veermans, and his craziness was blamed on his Portuguese-Sephardic descent. It made no difference that papa's family had been Mokummers since the early 17th century when they came to Holland after a long settlement in South America. As a result of the Spanish Inquisition of 1492 the Garcia family had fled from Portugal and eventually settled in South America. After a sojourn of almost a century in South America, they migrated to Amsterdam. The Veermans were Ashkenazi Jews who had lived in Amsterdam for probably a little less than a century after fleeing Polish or German pogroms; but to the Veermans the Garcias were somewhat eccentric outsiders.

My earliest boyhood memory is of being taken to visit my grandmother Veerman on the Jodenbreestraat. She lived in the house of one of her sons, my Oom Philip Veerman, and his wife, my Tante Rebecca. I visited my ancient grandmother in her sleeping cupboard off the kitchen. My age was four or five. During that time I looked forward every day to attending a Montessori kindergarten school in our neighborhood near the Van Woustraat.

We lived in a third floor walk-up apartment consisting of a living room, two bedrooms, a kitchen, a clothes closet, a water closet, and a dumbwaiter for hauling up our groceries and packages from the ground floor. Just as one took cake batter and bread dough out to be baked by a commercial baker, so one went to the neighborhood bathhouse on Smaragdstraat to take a bath. The bathhouse was at the other end of the street on which the private rowing club was housed, and behind the bathhouse were two primary schools, one of them mine.

One of the luxuries in our apartments was a radio-like box which could be tuned in to any of four stations by paying a monthly fee. My parents kept our radio tuned only to VARA, the Social Democrat station, about which my father was dogmatic. Mother tuned in to their programs of music when she was able to listen during the day. Both parents would listen in the evenings to political talks, opera, operettas and light music. I listened to very little of this until my teenage years when I began to enjoy the opera and operettas to which my parents were devoted. I remember switching the station to try out some American jazz one Saturday only to have my father insist I switch it back again to a familiar opera.

Papa encouraged me from an early age to establish some independence from the watchful eye of my mother. I played in ever-widening circles, coming to know the streets of our neighborhood well. As a very young boy my world extended from Saffierstraat to Van Woustraat to the Amstel River to the Josef Israels Kade (canal) to the Tolstraat, where my father worked in the Asscher Diamond Factory.

On Saturdays we boarded the No. 8 streetcar to the Jodenbreestraat to visit the families of one of mother's two brothers and several of her five sisters who lived on and around that street. We children looked forward to these visits and to being indulged with refreshments and an occasional *stuiver* by our relatives. Our streetcar rode on tracks straight down the center of the Jodenbreestraat, nosing with clanging bell through walkers and shoppers who spilled from the sidewalk onto the narrow street. We passed vendors' carts catering to knots of shoppers looking for bargains in groceries, clothing, and housewares. Horse and bicycle carts wove slowly behind and in front of the streetcar. A car or truck was only rarely seen. Friends stopped to visit in the shade of awning-covered shops, causing walkers to detour into the streets and slow traffic further.

We headed first for a visit with mother's brother, Oom Philip Veerman, and his wife, Tante Rebecca, a warm and colorful woman who had no children of her own. Oom Philip, a dapper dresser, owned a fairly prosperous poultry store, which both husband and wife helped maintain. When we called at their apartment I romped with their German shepherd dog, "Egon."

After a brief visit we walked next door and climbed a dark stairway to the second floor apartment of mother's closest sister, Tante Grietje, and her husband, Oom Meyer Rubens. Oom Meyer was a traveling salesman dealing in picture frames. Their one son, Hans, was five years older than I, too old for me to know well.

Across the street, we called on another sister of my mother, Tante Duifje, married to Oom Salomon Melkman, and their three children, Floortje, Anneke, and Broertje. The Melkmans, too, managed a prospering poultry business and, in the early days of these visits, lived upstairs from their shop. Duifje and Salomon were cheerful, hard-working people. Their daughters, Floortje and Anneke, were vivacious, and Floortje, the oldest, was always well-dressed and considered one of the prettiest girls in the Veerman tribe. The girls were six and five years older than I, but Broertje was my age and my closest cousin. While our parents visited, Broertje and I often played together in the streets or went to the movie theatre, dutifully taking with us my younger sister, whom we called by her nickname, Sienie.

One block over and down an alley was the Waterlooplein where the apartment of Oom Michel and mother's sister, Tante Klaartje de Lara, was located. Their four boys, Appie, Meyer, David, and Phillip were also older than I, but the two younger boys, David and Flip (as we called Philip), were often good company even though they were closer to Floortje's age than mine.

Oom Michel was my wealthiest uncle, a dealer in the feathers of geese, swans, ducks, and chickens, and in all kinds of pelts, such as rabbits, hares, cats, and moles.

His oldest son, Appie, worked as an accountant-manager of his father's business after completing his studies in accountancy. Meyer, the second son, also a young adult (and named, like me, after our grandfather Meyer Veerman), was studying to become a rabbi when I was a boy. In the fateful year of 1939, he was to know the honor of being appointed the rabbi of the Portuguese Sephardic Synagogue, of which our families were members.

Oom Michel owned some canalside warehouses full of feathers and pelts, and at times he hired me, a youngster, to work with my cousins David and Flip, doing odd jobs. Often we stood at the side of the canal before great mounds of pelts which we were required to flail, one by one, on the inner skin side in order to soften them up and clean them. As we worked we watched the working boats and barges as they slipped by us, exchanging quips and cracks with some of the families aboard them. Our noses were used to the ripe odors of the garbage scow tethered nearby. I was at home in my uncle's warehouse and liked being paid to work there, but the pelts had to be handled carefully and we took our work seriously. I was quite in awe of Oom Michel, not because he had money but because he had a huge belly which he carried before him with dignity. He was a short man and so rotund he could not bend far enough to tie his shoes.

There were other relatives on my mother's side with whom our relations were more distant. I hardly knew my mother's oldest sister, Rebecca, or her husband, Oom Gerrit Reens. Occasionally we visited another older sister, Tante Jetje, and Oom Folie Hekster. They had four children: two boys, two girls. Their oldest son, Meyer, was nearly my father's age and left in the early thirties for South Africa. Nico, their youngest and a son about six years older than I, chatted easily with me when our families visited. Just before the war he passed some examinations which earned him a coveted queen's scholarship for medical school. The Nazis occupied us soon afterwards, and Nico was not destined to start his higher schooling or even to live much longer.

Abraham, mother's oldest brother, was in some way

mentally deficient, and had to be taken care of, along with his wife and children, by all of the Veerman relatives.

My father's family was smaller and, as I have mentioned, not so close to us as mother's family. The men of his family had always been diamond polishers. Grandfather Judah Garcia and grandfather's brother had polished diamonds. My father, Elie, and his brother, Maurits, were both diamond polishers. Maurits and his wife had three children, two boys and a girl, and lived in the neighborhood of the Heksters. However, we barely knew them because my mother did not care for the company of Maurits' wife.

Father also had a sister, Jaantje, and Jaantje did not marry a diamond polisher. Her husband, Oom Aaron Delden, in partnership with his father and uncles, owned several shops specializing in bicycles, bicycle parts, electrical supplies and equipment. The Deldens had two boys, both younger than Sienie. They lived on the fringe of the Jewish section and stayed in close touch with my father though our families did not often exchange visits.

We Garcias belonged to the venerable Portugese Sephardic Synagogue, the interior of which Rembrandt had etched so carefully in the 17th century, recording for us comfortable proof that the interior did not change as did the congregations and their clothing styles. As a family, however, we were hardly devout, and rarely attended services on Saturday before setting forth to visit one or another of our relatives. We attended services on High Holy Days and on special occasions such as Bar Mitzvahs and weddings. Oom Michel de Lara and his son, Meyer— who would one day become the rabbi there—are remembered particularly among our family as devout members of the Portuguese Sephardic Synagogue.

My father had one ritual to which he looked forward every week: to join some of his fellow diamond workers for a Saturday morning game of whist and a good cigar at a restaurant on the Rembrandtsplein. It was our custom for our family to meet downtown, after papa's game of whist, and from there to visit our relatives.

One Saturday when I was six or seven years old,

mother dressed me up as usual in my best clothes, then sent me out to play as she and Sienie dressed. We were planning to take the streetcar to meet papa on the Jodenbreestraat after he finished his game. Outside I saw some of my friends running about in some apartment buildings under construction down the street, and I ran to join them. We followed one another through the open framing and up and down ramps. We began to dare one another to jump out of the second story window frames and into some piles of sand beneath. In no time we were all jumping waist-deep into the sand heaps which contained a chalky substance that whitened our clothes and our skin. When my mother saw the scene she was furious. She took me home to wash and redress me, scolding angrily, handling me roughly. We were late meeting my father, and I cringed as mother began to relate to him what I had done. I feared my father's anger, which could be swift and explosive. But instead of turning on me in anger, he laughed, throwing back his head. "Oh, Rozetje," he said, "don't be upset. Now I know I really have a boy!"

I liked school, putting in my first six years with the same classmates and the same teacher, Mevrouw van der Roest. These were my happiest years for I had close friends and a teacher who was both familiar and devoted. Mevrouw van der Roest grew to know her students extremely well, and we felt comfortable with her. A gentile, she taught a class of thirty children, half of them Jewish, shaping us into a receptive but disciplined group of students. She learned our weaknesses and our strengths, and helped us where we needed it most. She filled us with the excitement of learning and the desire to learn more. I remember at one point recovering from an illness that kept me out of school for more than a week. When I returned to class Mevrouw van der Roest took me home with her after school, fortified me with milk and cookies, then tutored me two hours a day until I caught up with my classmates.

We learned to swim in a new swimming complex called the Miranda Baths at the end of Rynstraat. As a swimmer

I started late and did not feel at home in the water. We had to pass some ability tests at the Miranda Baths, the worst of which, for me, being the mastering of the backstroke. Invariably I sank, and came up sputtering for air. I felt sure I was going to drown, but I finally passed the test when I realized my friends were finishing up the course and leaving me behind.

Skating on ice was more my sport. The Sint Niklaas Day when I received my first skates was the most exciting I remember. In Holland, even the Jewish children celebrated Sint Niklaas Day, which was a holiday especially for children, falling on December 5. Christmas for the gentiles was a religious holiday of major significance. Chanuka for the Jews was a minor religious holiday. Sint Niklaas Day was awaited with excitement by all children. Within our apartment building tension would build as the day neared. We sang traditional songs on Sint Niklaas Eve and placed our stockings, each containing a crisp carrot for the horse of "Sinterklaas," on the mantel over our stoves. Sinterklaas was the children's affectionate term for Sint Niklaas. After what seemed like hours, Sinterklaas arrived, and read to us awe-stricken children from his record book. He called each of us to account for some of our bad deeds which he had faithfully catalogued. We cried and promised never to do such things again. We were always forgiven, and then we all sang again as Sinterklaas handed around candy. Games were played and winners and losers alike received small gifts. After the celebration we received a gift or two from our parents That is how one year I received wooden skates and began learning to negotiate the Amstel and the city's canals.

Some years later I skated with my friends to the outlying villages of Ouderkerk and Diemen. We took lunch and some small change in order to buy hot soup and hot cocoa on the way. The bitter winter winds pushed us along or held us back when we reversed our direction. The delicious-smelling steam from soup and cocoa stalls along the ice enticed us as we exerted ourselves. We stopped on occasion to warm ourselves inside and out before steaming-hot cauldrons on pot-bellied stoves.

Amsterdam, then a city of about 750,000, had a Jewish population that was probably close to 100,000. Of this population only a few thousand were Orthodox Jews. We Jews chose to live near one another, but we were not forced to live so. Almost no one in the days before the occupation made an issue of the Jewish community. We were accepted as fellow Mokummers, and all of us townspeople got along on the basis of interests we held in common. Business transactions, the hobbies of housewives, the activities of school children led to many friendships between Jews and gentiles. A few Yiddish words made their way into the vernacular, such as *"smeris"* or *"shamus"* for "policeman." Amsterdam Jews came and went about town at will. By the time I was eleven, I was exploring my way around most of Amsterdam on my bicycle. Gradually I felt at ease in any part of the city I cared to look over.

My friends and I were great fans of American movies. The Saturday afternoon movies on the Centuurbaan became a way of life for us during the long afternoon visits of our parents. We jumped eagerly into new worlds with such romantic, if differing, fare as the films of Shirley Temple, Charlie Chaplin, Boris Karloff, Tom Mix, Laurel and Hardy, and Rin Tin Tin. The movies played in English with subtitles, enabling me to learn a few words and phrases. We were profoundly impressed with the seeming wealth of American city people, each with his own car and elaborately furnished home, his smart clothes changing with every scene. We were awestruck by the adventures waiting in the western hills for anyone foolhardy enough to leave the cities. In adolescence I fell under the spell of Fred Astaire and Ginger Rogers. I followed them worshipfully as they glided about opulent sets in tails and satins. In my mind I joined them, dancing off gracefully with a beautiful partner of my own.

I was growing old enough also to begin to understand some of the conversations of my parents with relatives and friends. I gradually learned that my father, regardless of his general good humor, had never really liked being a diamond polisher, and resented the fact that his own father had insisted that he stay in the family trade. There were bad feelings between father and son. My Antwerp grandfather was a devout Portuguese Jew, but religion sat more lightly on my father's shoulders. When papa was a very young man he had gone to England and, finding it to his liking, returned to ask grandfather's permission to move there and try his hand in business. Grandfather told him that he had to stay home and learn the family trade of diamond polishing first, that he could not drift around without a trade. Father learned the trade, beginning to earn money as his skills increased, and beginning to take interest in some local girls as his money increased. Within a couple of years he married my mother, and the dream of starting a new life in England was dead. I think he cherished the hope that I might make it in his place, however, and so he encouraged my independence and my easy facility for languages. He brought me English-language newspapers and insisted that I learn some English

As the depression deepened and more and more jobs were lost in the community, papa hit upon an idea for going into a new business. My father was basically a frustrated entrepreneur who dearly loved business. He went to see Oom Philip Veerman, his brother-in-law and poultry store owner, to ask his cooperation in allowing papa to open a branch-like poultry store in our own neighborhood. It would be supplied by Oom Philip and staffed by my father and mother for a percentage of the profits of Oom Philip. Philip agreed to try it, and so my father rented a garage, built a counter, some racks, and a storage shed in the back. There was even a kerosene heating lamp and an ice box. Located on Diamantstraat, the store opened up for afternoon business only, the time of day when people were in the habit of going out to make their purchase for the evening meal. Mother tended the store. My father continued to work at the diamond factory where layoffs were occurring with increasing frequency. Because a two-hour lunch was customary everywhere, even in the schools, we all gathered at the store for a mid-day meal together. Mother had our lunch ready when we arrived, and father cut up chickens while he ate. I was taught to help kill, cut up, and wrap chickens, then deliver them. It was a fascinating process. The chickens were slaughtered in a basement room under Oom Philip's store on the Jodenbreestraat. Access to the basement was by covered cellar steps to the left of the shop's front door. Live chickens delivered in crates were slid down a wooden chute placed over the steps. Oom Philip's employees would pull out the chickens, one by one, slit their throats and throw them hard against the blood-stained wall in order to stun them before they died. The plucking was done by expert hands, a chore of little more than five minutes' work per chicken. I was trained to help with all processes over the protests of my mother, who did not appreciate my bringing home chicken lice. Each time I worked in Oom Philip's cellar she sent me to the bathhouse while she washed my workclothes. Oom Philip occasionally rewarded me for helping with a gift of a cracked egg from which I would enthusiastically suck out the raw contents. During lunch and after school I helped in our store, learning to disembowel, clean, and cut up poultry. I delivered chickens on my bicycle to waiting housewives, who placed them in their veranda coolers or started their cooking immediately.

On cold days I found my mother tending the shop red nosed, bundled in sweaters, long underwear, and scarves. Most of the orders were standard each week. Sometimes neighbors ran into mother on the street and told her what they wanted. She took and filled orders conscientiously.

"Hey, Rozetje! I want you to put by a two-pound chicken for me for Friday noon."

"How are you, Rozetje! Will you please have Max deliver a half dozen eggs to me by five this afternoon."

Oom Salomon Melkman had a poultry shop diagonally across the street from Oom Philip's main store, and both, incidentally, were within a few doors of Rembrandt's historic house. Now when Oom Salomon saw how our branch store with Oom Philip was flourishing, he decided to open an extra store of his own about a block and a half away. Needless to say, the new store caused a bitter rift within the family. My father deeply resented Salomon's new store because he himself had formulated the idea and was succeeding with it. Now neither store had enough business. By now, too, my father's fears had been realized, and he had been laid off at the diamond factory. Just as we became solely dependent on the poultry store, our customers were growing poorer by the day. They could no longer afford to buy whole chickens, and began to order only a half or a quarter at a time. They purchased only two or three eggs a week. At least we had some food along with our tiny income even though we ate mostly chicken. It is a wonder that I still like chicken, but I do.

My father insisted that I read the works of Pieter Jelles Troelstra, the founder of our Dutch Social Democratic Labor Party and of *Het Volk,* the socialist newspaper to which we subscribed. Considered the father of social democracy in Holland, Troelstra had left a good legacy of reform legislation by the time he died in 1930. At the turn of the century he had represented the party in parliament, and had devoted himself to influencing social legislation ever since.

I joined the Social Democratic Youth Movement, which took girls as well as boys into its ranks, and attended their meetings and rallies in the blue shirt and red neckerchief that made up our uniform. Our activities were not much different from a co-educational scout troop, minus merit badges.

Economic conditions became precarious. My sister and I went about in hand-me-down clothing. We walked with my parents in an enormous national strike march near the Vondel Park. During the elections my father busied himself with the campaigns of the Social Democrats. One night he came home spattered with blood, and told my mother about fights in the streets with the Communists.

"Why is it any of your business?" mother screamed. "Let them alone, Elie! Stay out of it. Do you want to be killed?"

"If we don't stop them, who will?" papa shouted back.

My father left on a trip to Belgium—the year was 1935—and when he returned he announced we were moving to Antwerp where he had landed a job at a Belgian diamond plant.

We moved at night, along with a family named Prins, in a rented truck driven by a hired driver. Papa had already rented a modest apartment for us in Antwerp, and the following day we unpacked in unfamiliar surroundings.

Overnight my friends were gone and my life changed completely. I was 11 years old, a difficult time to lose the familiar surroundings of my brief lifetime. But there was no question that we must start again. My sister and I easily learned Flemish, a dialect of Dutch, and we finished up the last few months of the school year, for me the sixth grade. In the fall I started classes at the Meerdere Uitgebreid Lagere Onderwys (MULO), or middle school and equivalent to the American junior high school. I reached the school, which was on the opposite side of town, by means of a long streetcar trip. The MULO was a school for boys offering a rigid educational program. Few memories of the place stay with me except that it was the first school I attended that required my submitting to the services of a school dentist. For the first time in my life I was examined by a dentist and, as a result, put through some excruciating hours of tooth-filling and extraction. Dentists suddenly headed my list of people to avoid. The MULO took me efficiently through a standard curriculum including fluency in French, which was a necessity in bilingual Belgium.

During the summers that followed we took brief vacations to Holland. Months became years and I came to know Antwerp well. My father prospered in his work. We were able to move to a larger, modern apartment, complete with hot water, bathroom with shower, and even a telephone. Our neighborhood was made up almost exclusively of Dutch migrant diamond workers. Wages were generally lower in Antwerp than they had once been in Amsterdam, but the industry was still in full operation.

I have mentioned that my grandfather Judah Garcia

lived in retirement in Antwerp with his second wife and performed duties as a *shamus* in a small synagogue there. But papa and grandfather still did not heal the rift between them, and we did not live near one another. Nevertheless, when I began studying for my Bar Mitzvah near the age of 13, I was sent for training to my grandfather. There was little joy in the process. He was strict, and I was not attracted by my grandfather's orthodoxy.

There was not much joy in the actual ceremony either. The Bar Mitzvah was held in an impersonal walk-up temple in a converted office building rather than our ancient Portuguese Sephardic Synagogue in Amsterdam where my father's Bar Mitzvah had been celebrated and those of many other male relatives and ancestors. Our family was pleased to entertain Tante Grietje, Tante Rebecca, and Tante Duifje, who had traveled by bus to Antwerp to attend the ceremony, but none of us were happy to be so far from home for this momentous occasion.

1937—1939

In Belgium and Holland schooling was not mandatory after the age of 13. In my family it had long been a necessary practice to drop school and go to work at the legal age. I took it for granted, then, that following my Bar Mitzvah and the finishing up of my spring semester at the MULO in 1937, I would accompany my father to the factory and begin apprenticing as a diamond polisher. The knowledge of my father's own dissatisfaction with his trade warmed a certain reluctance in me to follow in his footsteps; yet I saw no alternative to my fate.

I nurtured some secret daydreams, however, about a

private ambition that had sprung to life on one of our recent vacation trips to Holland. There I had met an attractive and sophisticated young lady from southern Holland of about my age. In a matter of moments she had turned my mind upside down when she began to tell me of her plans to become a licensed pharmacist. A pharmmacist! And she...a girl! She asked me what I planned to do with my life. I was taken by surprise but knew I could not tell this girl with whom I was rapidly becoming infatuated that I had never thought about my life as my own to control. I cast about quickly in my mind and remembered my talent for sketching, for which Mevrouw van der Roest used to take me to task as a sign of day-dreaming. At the same time I had a sudden insight into how much I had loved returning to Amsterdam and looking about at her buildings, old and new, many of them bearing cornerstone inscriptions to the effect that they were erected by the design of Architect So-and-So in such-and-such a year. I confessed to her that I hoped to become an architect and watched her beam approvingly just as if I had not made a perfectly outlandish statement. Such was the moment of my first dawning thoughts on directing myself toward a profession I so greatly respected. I began to look at buildings with increasing awareness, noticing with satisfaction that sedate contemporary buildings could live in interesting harmony with medieval neighbors.

But here was I back in Antwerp, and my father introduced me at the factory. I was greeted warmly as the son of Elie Garcia. The teacher assigned for my apprenticing was a goliath, over six feet tall and big in the shoulders. We sat opposite each other at his table. During the ensuing months he revealed to me gradually the slow, tedious steps of the polishing process. I was allowed to progress in these steps according to my mastery of each one. The work was dust-producing as well as monotonous. Eventually, I adjusted, learned, and progressed. I discovered I had a good three-dimensional sense and could quickly perceive the facets of a diamond. My basic allowance money of a few francs began to grow with my skill. I took home ever larger amounts to my mother, who gave me in return an allowance for my weekly needs.

At the age of 14½ years, I cracked a very large stone. I gave it to my teacher who exploded and called me a variety of depressing names. My own anger boiled up. I turned abruptly and walked silently to my locker, changed clothes, and headed for the door.

"Where the hell do you think you're going, Max? I haven't dismissed you yet."

"I don't care whether you dismiss me or not. I'm quitting," I answered. "I don't want to be a diamond polisher."

"And what do you think you're going to do with yourself if you can't make it as a diamond polisher?"

"I'm going to become an architect!" I shot back foolishly.

"Aha! You hear that? You hear that, everybody?" he shouted around the room. "Max Garcia is going to become an architect. And where is your father going to find the money to send you to the university? Where do you get these hair-brained ideas?"

I turned back to the door and walked out.

"How come you are home so early, Max? Are you sick?" my mother asked, advancing anxiously to search my face. When I explained what happened she started to cry. "Oh, what's to become of you, Max? What's your father going to say? Architect? Architect? What's this all about?" She continued to quiz me through her tears until papa walked in.

The word, it seemed, had spread like flame through the factory rooms that Max Garcia had cracked a stone and had quit, that he had further boasted that he was going to become an architect. At least my father was prepared for what he would find when he arrived home.

"Rozetje, I've heard," he told mother as she began to explain my disaster. "Look, Max, this is a serious matter. Tell me now, what is this everyone is telling me about your quitting and about wanting to become an architect?"

Without telling him about the challenge of the girl, I told him about my realization on our last trip to Amsterdam that I would like to study to become an architect. "Papa," I pleaded, "I know it is not possible at this time for me to go to the university, but it is my dream to be able to try one day. One thing I am sure of, I don't want to be a diamond polisher."

My father looked at me for a long time, and asked me if I understood I would have to work long and hard to be able to earn the money for school, assuming that I could study enough to pass the entrance examinations. After dinner, my polishing teacher, who lived in the neighborhood, came over to talk to my father about me. I was soon called into the living room and my teacher apologized for his outburst. He confessed that a hairline crack had been visible in the stone when he gave it to me and that he should have brought it to my attention. He realized he had expected too much of me to assume that I would notice it and polish it accordingly so that the crack would not show. He apologized for that too, and I accepted his apology.

"Come on back with us, Max," my teacher offered. "You've been doing a reliable job, and if you continue you should be due for a raise."

"No," I replied, "I meant what I said this afternoon. I do not want to try diamond polishing again, and I do not want to return to the factory."

There was a silence before my father spoke. "If Max does not want to continue with diamond polishing, I will not make him. Let him see what else he can do with himself."

That was that. I did not return to the factory except to pick up my belongings.

The streets became a lonely learning place as I drifted about jobless, hating to return home to face my worried mother. I did not fail to look well at Antwerp's age-blackened buildings and the handsome contemporary apartments of my own neighborhood as well. I learned my way around the districts and neighborhoods of Antwerp almost as well as I knew my way around Amsterdam.

Within a couple of weeks I found temporary work with a

butcher, helping to make sausages. I stuffed intestine casings with a mixture of raw meat, peppers, and spices, preparing them to send out to the smokehouse, a job I enjoyed learning. When we had made a generous supply of sausages the butcher no longer needed me, and I approached my father for permission to take a vacation trip home to Amsterdam on my bicycle, a distance of about 150 kilometers. I was often homesick for the town of my birth, and longed for a chance to visit relatives and childhood friends. Such a bicycle trip by a boy my age was unheard of, and my mother began to make a great fuss. Papa, however, turned the idea over in his mind for awhile, then agreed to let me go.

Mother wrote in furious resignation to Tante Grietje, Tante Rebecca, and Tante Duifje to expect me by bicycle because of the foolhardy plot of the mad father and the mad son. Mother's sisters wrote or telephoned back agreeing with mother's objection to this dangerous trip. Nevertheless my parents managed to set a date for my relatives to expect me in Amsterdam, and I left on schedule early one morning with a small packet of food and a few changes of clothes. I was a little uneasy at first as I pedaled along the bicycle path beside the main highway, but I kept a good pace and stopped only once when I had to fix a flat—a routine affair. As I recognized the outskirts of Amsterdam my exhilaration grew; and entering the town in the early evening, I rode proudly and directly to my aunt's house.

I stayed for about two weeks, wandering happily about my hometown, visiting friends and relatives, accepting without question their generous hospitality in keeping and feeding me. I was allowed to return to Antwerp on my bicycle with none of the family hysteria that accompanied my initial trip. My father, mother, and sister were a welcome sight when I arrived home. Yet my trip had been an exciting adventure that greatly boosted my self-confidence. My father was proud of me for undertaking it, I could tell. My mother began to understand that she was no longer to look upon me as a helpless boy. Her boy was reaching for manhood.

I worked at odd jobs until the late spring of 1939 when my father decided that we should return to Holland. To shed some light on the reasoning behind his decision, I will retrace a bit of history in very broad terms.

In 1936, Germany remilitarized the Rhineland, a territory taken from the defeated Germans by French and Belgian forces in World War I, and administered under terms of the Versailles Treaty. The Rhineland territory was fully restored to Germany by 1930 with the stipulation that the Germans maintain no fortifications or military equipment within the area. The Rhineland was of considerable importance to Germany because of its coal resources and iron and steel mills in both Ruhr and Saar districts, as well as rich agricultural and wine-growing regions. Belgium touched on a northern border of industrial sections of the Rhineland, and when Hitler moved in troops, Belgian newspapers screamed the bad news.

In 1938, there was the "Anschluss," as Hitler quickly annexed Austria, which move, in turn, set up the partial isolation of Czechoslovakia. The Sudetenland was also taken in 1938. Czechoslovakia capitulated in 1939. Memel, at Germany's northeast border, was retaken in 1939. Hungary, Rumania, and the Balkans were left independent but vulnerable from both east and west.

My parents and their friends were outraged that the governmental strategists of England and France seemed to be burying their heads in the sand rather than trying to check the drift of Germany's reawakened militarism. My father came to realize that the situation would continue to deteriorate unchecked, that war was imminent, and that he had better look to protecting his family as best he could. Remembering the strategies of World War I, father believed that the Germans would probably repeat their invasion of Belgium in order to get to France without trying to penetrate the Maginot Line. Holland, he figured, might just be safe again and left as neutral territory. No matter what happened we would surely be better off in our own country as Dutch citizens.

My father returned to Amsterdam, obtained a diamond polishing job back at the Asscher plant, and rented an apartment for us on Graaf Florisstraat. The three of us then followed by bus, and our family was divided up and placed around with relatives until our furniture could be shipped and our apartment set up.

I stayed with Tante Duifje because her son Broertje and I were friends. On the night before my 15th birthday in late June, the telephone rang for me. It was my father calling to tell me that on my birthday he was going to let me accompany the driver of a rented truck to Antwerp to oversee the moving of our possessions to Graaf Florisstraat. He told me he considered me a man now, and that I even had his permission to smoke.

The driver and I traveled by truck back over the road to Antwerp, and once there I directed him to our apartment. We tackled each room, packing boxes, loading furniture, working like field horses in order to return the truck next day to Amsterdam. Back on Graaf Florisstraat, the work was even harder, as every box and piece of furniture had to be unloaded, then hoisted by pulley through a third-story window. Within two days our family was reunited in our furnished apartment. I was proud to have been called on and to have been able to help so responsibly.

By July I had hired out as a stevedore at a dockside warehouse. I recall one strange duck there who sent me out every day to the baker for a cream puff for his lunch. It was not long before I traded in my laboring job for a chance to work at a travel agency where I hoped I could eventually put my drawing ability to some use and try my hand at advertising layout. I did routine paste-up jobs there, envelope stuffing, and typical backroom work, but the atmosphere was pleasant, and associating, even peripherally, with world travel seemed glamorous.

Our work came to a standstill on Friday, September 1, 1939, when word swept into our office that Germany had attacked Poland. For the next few days everyone was in a state of suspended motion. Listening to and passing on radio reports was about all that was accomplished. I was required to work on Sundays and it was a Sunday, September 3, that England and France declared war on Germany. We closed up and ran out into the streets to join a milling crowd that grew ever larger. The travel business withered almost overnight and, once again, I was out of a job.

1939—1942

We stayed close to our radio for news reports and pored over our newspaper, *Het Volk*, for detailed bulletins. Direct reports from England and France reached us through short-wave radios of our wealthier friends and relatives. Oom Aaron Delden, whose wife was father's sister, Jaantje, and who now owned several electrical stores, put speakers up outside his radio shop on the Vyselstraat. I would stop by to stand with great knots of listeners to hear the latest direct news bulletins.

Following the attack on Poland, protest rallies sprang up one after another all over town. The Dutch Nazi party, which had been swelling in numbers and activity in recent years, was now openly attacked by the left and communist elements. Everyone we knew was in a state of nerves, recalling the severe shortages and disruptions of World War I, and wondering how soon we would be in for more of the same or worse. Did we face conquest and occupation? What then? We drew even closer to our relatives, getting together with related families whenever time could be found. Among the adults there was speculation about what might be in store for Dutch Jews in the event of occupation. We were aware of the large number of German Jewish refugees among us already and of the reasons for their flight from Germany. At this time my father was 43 years old, my mother 44, my sister almost 13, and I, 15.

Poland fell within a very few weeks, after which all fronts became ominously quiet. The loudest noises to be heard were the propaganda broadsides between opposing nations. We tried to concentrate on our daily lives. Oom Aaron gave me a job in one of his electrical stores. I performed miscellaneous stockroom chores and often acted as a messenger-carrier between stores located on the Haarlemmer Dyk, the Van der Pekstraat, and the Plantage Middellaan. The Plantage Middellaan was a beautiful wide street, lined with trees, a major artery leading to and from the Jewish section, and I liked working there. Tante Klaartje and Oom Michel lived on a side street near Oom Aaron's shop, and I sometimes stopped by to see them and to accept refreshments. When my parents heard about these workday visits, however, they put a stop to them with a stern lecture. I was not to take up my relatives' time or look forward to refreshments from them on weekdays. I was reminded that they had four sons of their own to look after.

During the winter the Nazi war machine was quiet. Only the war of nerves was loud, fed by rumor and propaganda. As the months passed, our tensions built up because we expected a spring offensive. The army reserves were called to active duty. Holland prepared for her own defense, initiating plans for breaking dikes and flooding southern portions of the country from the Zuider Zee all the way to Zeeland in order to create a wide moat against enemy onslaught. The Dutch Nazis were watched and catalogued as a 5*th*-column organization, though political freedom in Holland continued to guarantee them unrestricted movement. The German government broadcast promises to honor Dutch sovereignty, and vehemently denied rumors of German intentions to invade.

On the evening of May 10, 1940, however, with strong protestations that Holland had betrayed her neutrality as a nation, the German Army invaded us. Unknown to us, Denmark, Belgium, and Luxembourg were invaded at the same time. German armies moved swiftly into Holland just as they did into our neighboring small countries. The dreaded spring offensive was upon us. Many Dutch fascists were rounded up. The dikes were broken as planned, and whole areas inundated but German planes full of paratroopers and equipment flew over the flooded areas, confounding Dutch defenses. Work came to a standstill. Reserves were ordered into action overnight. The Dutch Army set up defensive positions. German paratroopers in civilian clothing dropping behind our moat became a formidable threat. They linked up with undercover Dutch fascists who were still at large, and seized key locks and water control points. On the third day of the war the Nazis issued an ultimatum that Holland surrender immediately or Rotterdam would be bombed. The ultimatum was ignored and Rotterdam was severely bombed. Holland surrendered soon thereafter to protect her other cities from similar devastation. The conquest of our country took five days. The queen fled to England, and set up a government in exile.

During those few days of war, my father had walked the neighborhood as air raid warden while my mother draped windows and waited anxiously with my sister and me. During the day we began to encounter Dutch Army roadblocks which were set up throughout the city to catch German paratroop infiltrators. Whoever walked the streets was challenged to pronounce clearly various words that only Dutch born people could properly enunciate, such as "Scheveningen," "Schravenhage," "schelvis." Anyone whose pronunciation was faulty was detained for further questioning. The German Jews who were living in exile among us quickly learned to stay in their houses rather than risk being picked up as German spies.

Within a week we were a conquered people. We watched the German troops march through Amsterdam, entering from the direction of Utrecht and coming down the Amstellan a few blocks away. Though my mother had begged me to stay home, I could not resist running into the street and crossing the bridge to watch. Dutch fascists and German sympathizers came back into the streets in black uniforms. As the troops passed by they sent up their right arms: "Heil Hitler! Heil Hitler!" This proved to be premature in our just-conquered city because these same sympathizers were badly beaten that night when the parading was over, and the next morning numerous bodies were found in the canals.

Gradually the occupying forces became organized, and such acts of defiance were dared by fewer and fewer townspeople once stringent punishments were administered as the price of disobedience. Proclamations were issued to the effect that Dutch civil authorities would remain in control, that people were to continue as usual with their work. Everyone went back to work but no element of our lives went "back to normal." German troops and trucks were all over town. A system of registration was begun, followed immediately by food rationing.

Our Social Democratic party newspaper, *Het Volk*, was forced to cease publication and our political radio station, VARA, was silenced. Dutch citizens were forbidden, on pain of severe punishment, to listen to unauthorized broadcasts. Radio Free Holland and Radio Free England, which were broadcast from England, were expressly forbidden.

Rules multiplied and were strictly enforced. Dutch Nazis were elevated to official positions, including Burgermeester, operating as front men for the occupying forces. The Jews were not yet treated much differently from the rest of the occupied population except for having to endure a well-nurtured campaign of anti-Semitism.

By the latter part of 1940, Jews were beginning to experience cruel discrimination. Jews in civil and government jobs, college professors and school teachers were being dismissed. In February of 1941 the dock workers instituted a strike which they tried to widen throughout the city in protest of a street round-up of some Jews in the Jewish section. Jews had been picked up at random as hostages, beaten, and sent off to a German concentration camp in retaliation for some Nazi-provoked violence of a previous day. The workers' strike was a protest in the name of the Dutch people against the Nazi treatment of Dutch Jews. The strike seemed a wonderful victory to us Jews; however, our victory was short-lived because the

Nazis threatened to pick up hundreds more Jews if the strike continued. It ended in two days, and was publicized in the press as Jew-incited. More repressive measures followed.

Dutch industry changed considerably. Much of it, including the diamond industry, was forced to regear toward industrial production for the German war effort. My father's work became an essential wartime industry, which was fortunate because Jews in unessential work were being deprived of their jobs or businesses in ever-increasing numbers. As his factory regeared production, papa called me to his side one evening and told me to come back to work in the diamond factory. As your father and a Jew, he advised me, now is a time to seek safety, not dreams.

Once again I accompanied my father to work, and actually it was a relief to do so. Our new neighborhood was on the other side of the Amstel, and this necessitated our taking a little rowboat ferry to and from work at the old Asscher factory on Tolstraat. I worked on another floor from that of my father and, again, under a teacher. Picking up quickly on my earlier training, I moved swiftly in my apprenticeship. My small earnings began to increase. My father and I enjoyed taking the ferry home for two-hour lunches with my mother and sister.

Times were anxious. There was now a curfew for Jews. Our prospects looked gloomier by the day, but I did not forget my personal dream. I had bought a few architectural books, and since the curfew confined us to our homes at night, I pored for hours over the texts. There was a volume on the history of architecture, and there were handbooks of technical details then being used in Holland.

During some of my free daytime hours, I roamed the streets studying details of various buildings, old and new, that had been mentioned in my texts. I took a new proud interest in the Asscher Factory where we worked when I read of its design by a distinguished Dutch architect, and studied, first hand, the features mentioned in my book. The new brick apartment housing on Saffierstraat, the similar modern housing in which we had lived in Antwerp, the Miranda Baths swimming complex: these projects took on significance as I realized that they were part of the new social planning being evolved by architects of my own time. My father's Social Democratic party had raised the funds for some of this housing. I delighted in noting the unending variety of the brick design work in these structures. From afar, blocks of apartment looked uniform, orderly. On closer inspection each brick complex had its own motif, its own song to sing.

When my sister, Sippora, reached the age of 14 in November, 1940, she too was removed from school and put to work. Sippora became a seamstress in a small sewing atelier, or workshop, within the Jewish section on the other side of the Professor Tulpplein. Her shop made uniforms and other clothing for the German Army.

Inflation ballooned and rationing tightened. An active black market sprang up in foods and goods no longer available to the Dutch population. My father jumped into this market as into an exciting new adventure. He enlisted some Dutch police officers as contacts, who, in turn were in touch with other black marketeers and the underground. He began to buy and sell coffee, cheeses, and the like, eventually doing very well for himself. Dad and his accomplices knew that they must not be caught, and so they stuck with known contacts.

He worked out a trade in black-market cheeses with a farmer he knew down the Amstel River. In this enterprise I was invited to lend a hand. We rode our bicycles after work and on weekends down the Amstel River to the farm where we each picked up a couple of great wheels of uncured cheese and concealed them in our saddle bags for the ride back. Once back home we carried the cheeses up the three floors to our flat where we placed them on boards in the closets. Every day the cheeses were turned over until they were completely cured. My father sold them whole or in part to those who could afford to buy. He delivered his orders by bicycle, usually to the wealthier sections of town. Looking back, I have to laugh at our black-marketing caper. The whole house reeked of cheese. All of our apparently trustworthy neighbors could not help but know about it. The bicycle trips down the Amstel with my father were like holidays. Sometimes we made a family outing of our cheese expeditions when my mother and sister accompanied us by bicycle on weekends and brought back extra cheeses.

My mother could now afford to buy cocoa and coffee and such otherwise unavailable delicacies when she wanted them. There was little else to buy besides basic necessities, so my father began to spend the extra guilders he was earning on stamp collections. He reasoned that they were a good investment and easy to conceal. A good number of months later when the pogroms against the Jews began in earnest, father turned these collections over to one of his police-officer associates for safekeeping. He also instructed me as to exactly where they were.

It was not until the spring of 1942 that we Jews were ordered to wear the yellow star patch inscribed "Jood" on our outer clothing. From this indignity there was no appeal. When we first appeared in public, marked as ordered, we were heartened that a number of our non-Jewish, working-class neighbors donned the star in sympathy. But this protest was swiftly put to an end as these protestors were threatened with having to register as Jews or be imprisoned for misrepresenting their identities.

With stars duly affixed to our chests, we were then easily subjected to curfews and, for many of us, an unaccustomed ghettoizing. No Jew was allowed on the streets after dark. Jews could shop the stores only at certain hours. Restaurants, movie houses, theatres, and concert halls were forbidden to Jews. All Jewish creative works from books to music were banned to the general public while the Jews were permitted to partake only of the Jewish culture. Jews could no longer be treated in non-Jewish hospitals or buy drugs from a non-Jewish pharmacy. Our separation from the rest of the population of Amsterdam became almost total. We now had to travel quite a distance to the Jewish section for prescription drugs. We associated now only with Jews, fearing for their sakes and ours to visit openly with one-time gentile friends.

A legitimate Jewish theatre sprang up on the Plantage Middellaan. This was not a Yiddish theatre but a true Dutch Jewish theatre, organic and spontaneous, interpreting our experiences. The theatre featured some distinguished talent, and was popular with all of us. We attended the Jewish symphony as well, and listened to a limited repertoire of music composed only by Jews but played with inspiration by a fine orchestra, many of whose members were former Concertgebouw players. I was particularly impressed by my introduction to the Jazz innovations of "Rhapsody in Blue," composed by an American Jew, George Gershwin. It is ironic to reflect that this period awakened the sensitivities of us working-class children to the wealth and variety of Jewish cultural life. The movie houses, once an entertainment mainstay, but now closed to us, were replaced by far more rewarding entertainment alternatives.

1942—1943

Shortly after her 16th birthday in November of 1942—my sister, Sienie, was still working as a seamstress alongside the new, young wife of my cousin, Hans Rubens, at the uniform plant in the Jewish section. As did my father and I and other working Jews, Sienie carried with her at all time her cherished work permit, which permitted Jews engaged in essential work to pass on the streets. One evening, however, Sienie did not return from work at the usual time and mother was just beginning to get alarmed when friends rushed in to tell her that Sienie and Hans Rubens' wife had been picked up with other Jewish workers in a street raid in that area. My father and I walked in our front door to find mother in hysterics.

Mother managed to tell us the story of what she had heard, but she could not believe that Sienie, with her work permit, had been picked. My parents reasoned that the incident had been a terrible mistake. Leaving me to calm mother, papa ran to the police station to try to get Sienie back. Papa pleaded for hours with a whole bureaucracy of authorities, but to no avail. He learned that the Nazis had raised the drawbridges over the canals surrounding the Jewish section and had picked up Sienie's group near their atelier on a canal on the other side of the Diamond Exchange. Experience was to teach us that this was one of the early calculated raids in which Jews were rounded up at random on the streets, permits or no. Families were torn apart and were afraid to start strong resistive measures for fear of retaliation against their captured members. It was not long before many families we knew had lost someone dear to this diabolical game of psychological roulette. No word of my sister's fate ever did come back to us.

At home my mother screamed and screamed, and tried to throw herself out of the window. My father became very worried, knowing he could no longer leave her alone. He enlisted neighbors and aunts to take turns looking after mother while we continued to go to work. Mother's mind gradually deteriorated after the disappearance of Sienie, and my father no longer laughed or joked.

Not knowing what next was in store for any of us Jews, we grimly continued to go to work. Many an evening papa and I raced our bicycles as usual down the Amstel on our cheese-smuggling expeditions in order to make it back home by curfew hour. We felt very close on those rides. In spite of mother's condition papa tried to stay rational. He was intent upon putting aside as much money as possible against the growing uncertainties of our future. In spite of great risks, he continued to deliver black market cheese. Daily we faced unknowable hazards, and our lives became miserably anxious.

Though we lived outside the Jewish section, we were

registered along with other Jewish neighbors, and our neighborhood began to feel the terror of unexpected raids. Having learned over the months about the Nazis' strange passion for official documents, my father obtained a stamped document from a doctor certifying that I was a chronic sufferer of migraine headaches. Indeed, I had suffered from severe headaches occasionally for many years. In my ninth year my mother had taken me to a doctor who had diagnosed the headaches as migraine.

Papa tacked the doctor's certificate to the door to my bedroom, and told me to be ready to take to my bed at a moment's notice with a feigned migraine attack. When the Nazis were heard on our street and we knew the inevitable raid was about to descend on us, papa had me drink a few slugs of Jenever from a bottle he had bought in order to bring on a headache. I then lay down on my narrow bed in the darkened bedroom I had shared until recently with my sister. I heard the approach of boots through our halls and my father's voice talking with the raiders. Then papa was calling attention to the document affixed to my door. The door swung open and I heard everyone troop in to look at me as I lay on the bed with eyes closed. It is hard for me to believe today that they walked out again and left me to my headache which, by then, was very real and which persisted for several day afterwards.

My parents were shaken by my narrow escape and began to look into ways to place me in hiding. Mother became more alert, and encouraged father to find a place for me to go. After many weeks of maneuvers, my father managed to secure a hiding place for me through the underground. A network of underground workers served as a conduit to families willing to hide Jews. It was understood that Jewish families would pay the costs of boarding those to be hidden. False documents and ration cards also had to be paid for. I do not know how much it cost my parents to secure a family to take me in and to have the necessary papers forged, but they used much of our black market savings to pay what was asked.

In early 1943, I dropped out of sight at work and in my

neighborhood. I went to a house, as instructed, where a family took me into their third-floor flat. I do not remember their names. They were a middle-aged couple with two sons near my own age. The father was Jewish and had to wear a star, but the mother was gentile. Her children had been brought up as Christians and did not have to register as Jews. (In Holland, Jews of mixed marriages and their offspring were often spared if they claimed to be converts. They were spared apparently because of official confusion and disagreement about what should be done about them.) My father had known my new guardian as a diamond-worker and as a former socialist colleague. In addition, he was a past chess master of Holland.

My new home was in Amsterdam East, a gentile working-class neighborhood. I lived with these people, a voluntary prisoner, not permitted to leave the house or even go near the windows. For a boy who had once roamed the streets of Amsterdam with total independence, this self-enforced restriction to quarters was extremely difficult. Actually, very few Mokummers were on the streets any longer without good reason, and definitely not if their families harbored a Jewish member. Thus, all of us found ourselves restricted to the house, and we entertained one another with games, or read, or listened to the radio. The former chess master taught me the rudiments of chess, which I had never before played, then some of the intricacies of strategy as my game developed.

I was hidden before my father finished his negotiations to obtain my false identity papers. The process took a number of months. When the papers arrived, the mistress of the household accompanied me out of the house and downtown for the first time of my stay with her family. She took me to a photographer who was considered trustworthy to take my identity picture. Once my papers were in order, my family began to drill me relentlessly about my new identity.

What's your name? Where were you born? What's your father's age? Your mother's maiden name? Where do you live? What's your birthday? Every day at odd moments someone would pop a question at me, and my responses had to be automatic. I did not forget the answers, even though I have forgotten them now.

I had brought with me my architectural and technical books. To help me in the study of these, my father had also subscribed for me to a correspondence course in architectural drawing. I worked for long periods on course assignments, then mailed them off, using the name of one of the sons.

My father sneaked up to see me on occasion, a trip of great personal risk since he had to remove his star and hope he would not be challenged for an inspection of his papers. With both children gone, mother's mental condition had continued to worsen, and father could not disguise his own depression in telling me this and other news. Mother sent heart-breaking messages of love. I missed them both very much, and wept with my father as we talked. Many members of our family had already been picked up. Papa went over with me exactly where our few valuables were hidden.

One nightmarish day the news was brought to me that my parents had been picked up in a neighborhood sweep. The news was not unexpected. Many other relatives and friends had been picked. The disappearance of Jews had become routine. But my father and mother disappearing was almost more than I could cope with. I tried to bear my grief silently. My "family" understood and tried to comfort me. My grief was a great block within me. Tears did not come, except sometimes in the night when my inner numbness gave way to despairing wailing.

The family and I continued to study, read, and play chess. I was not to realize until many years later that my parents had given me far more than their love and their savings to try to insure that I, at least, could be spared. I was to be reborn many times on the strength of their parenting. My mother had been attentive and affectionate. She had kept me firmly rooted and busy in our family and community. My father encouraged my independence and my abilities. He had been pleased to have me learn my way around the city. He had approved my bicycle trip from Antwerp to Amsterdam and back. He had assigned me the moving of the family furniture from one city to another. He had allowed me to try to change my status as a diamond worker.

Every time I recall having yelled, "It's been a long time since I had a *Lucky Strike*," to a liberating American tank crewman, I thank my father for teaching me to think on my feet and for insisting I learn some English. That yelled phrase changed the course of my life.

Again, I thank my father for sharing with me his gift of humor. The ability to laugh, even in desperate situations, is as good for life as food and drink. To cry is to feel worse. I know. I have wept copious tears and suffered great headaches and great depressions. To laugh is to feel better. I prefer laughter. I make an effort to laugh.

JUNE 1943

Night air raids on Germany had begun by the summer of 1943. The Allies, on one occasion in early June, apparently plotted their course to Germany through Amsterdam East where some key German war plants were situated. These plants were bombed one June night by Allied planes. When the air raid sirens ceased, our whole neighborhood ran out of their houses to watch great fires leaping in the distance where the plants had once stood. I joined the milling crowd before the Germans arrived to chase us all back inside.

Some nights later, after dinner, I heard cars on the street below. Glancing down through the curtains, one of the sons saw the Gestapo pulling up.

"There's the Gestapo."

"Max, get to the roof! Hurry!"

I skipped up the steps to the roof, tore across it, and hid

behind a skylight on the far side. Sure enough, the Gestapo was looking for me. They searched the house thoroughly but could find no trace of me since I could and did wear the clothes of the sons. Two gestapo agents finally came up the stairs to the roof. I saw the strong beams of their flashlights illuminating every detail along the roof line, including my skylight. But the agents did not cross the roof. They retreated back down the stairs. I remained crouched behind the skylight in the still night air, hardly daring to breathe, for what seemed a very long time. Finally, I was called back down and told that I would have to leave the house at once because somebody must have betrayed my presence. A few things were packed for me, including some money, and we parted with feelings that could be seen in one another's eyes but could hardly be expressed in words.

I was on the street before I could collect my thoughts. Where could I go? Numbly, I faced the next step. I recalled that cousin Hans Rubens had showed me where Tante Grietje and Oom Meyer kept the key to their apartment on Van Woustraat. I was aware that they had been picked up long since. Following a strong hunch that the key would still be there, I made my way cautiously through the night streets the considerable distance to their apartment. Just as I had hoped, the key was in its hiding place. I opened the door and walked in. The place was deserted but appeared eerily as it must have on the day my relatives had hurriedly left it. I took up residence, helping myself to supplies and using the place as my own, risking trips outside only for needed food. On the streets I carried with me my false identity card. My days alone at the apartment stretched into seeming weeks, but, in truth, I had lost track of time. The nights came early, with the failing of outside light, for I did not dare put on interior lights.

I began to make elaborate plans to escape by bicycle to Belgium, then through France to Switzerland, using my assumed identity. Papa had told me that my bicycle had been entrusted to friends on Graaf Florisstraat. I went to see them about it and to ask access to my parents' apartment. The Garcia apartment had been sealed to entrance they told me, but they also assured me my bicycle would be ready whenever I needed it. I returned then to the Rubens apartment and dawdled further over my plans for escape. I did not want to admit to myself how truly hopeless I felt about the trip. I was spared further efforts to ready plans and supplies and to work up courage to push off by the ringing of the doorbell one early afternoon. At first I did not answer it, but when the ringing persisted, I opened the door.

"You're Max Garcia," stated one of the two Dutchmen in civilan clothes.

"No, I'm so and so," I replied, using my assumed name.

"No, you're Max Garcia. What are you doing here?"

"You can see I am living here. Here are my papers if you want to see them."

"You are under arrest, Max Garcia. Come with us."

They marched me off without ceremony, taking me by automobile to the Jewish Theatre on the Plantage Middellaan. The theatre had been transformed into a collection place for Jews who were, I was told, to be sent to Westerbork, a work camp in northeastern Holland, near Groningen.

There I was interrogated by Dutch Nazis. At first I maintained that my false identity was my correct one. They insisted that they had proof that I was Max Rodriguez Garcia, a Sephardic Jew, and the son of Elias and Rosette Rodriguez Garcia. I capitulated. Yes, I was Max Rodriguez Garcia. Where had I been keeping myself all this time, they wanted to know. I told them I had moved about from place to place. They wanted more specifics and I made up a few places where I might have hidden. Where had I obtained my false identity papers, they wanted to know. I told them that I got papers through the underground, made up a rendezvous place, but maintained I knew no names. They worked at trapping me into changing answers but I stuck to my story. They released me then and threw me into the theatre-auditorium-turned-prison, which was filled with Jews.

The seats had been removed. I tried to stake out a small place for myself on the crowded floor. I spent my

19th birthday toward the end of June, 1943, in that place. We could hardly clean ourselves, and we smelled unwashed. Water was in short supply. We were fed regularly, but the meals were unappetizing. Little did I know that there would soon come a day when I would remember those meals as generous and good.

Our stay of a few weeks at the theatre ended when we were carted off in trucks directly to the railroad yards and herded into boxcars that were then sealed. I had noted that ours was not a railroad line to Westerbork, but I did not know where we were headed. Our car was jammed with men, women, and children. A single can for relieving ourselves stood in one corner, the only amenity conceded, and that a mockery, it turned out, as the days went by. We carried with us rations of food and water that each of us was given for the trip. We were also allowed to bring with us whatever other supplies and valuables we had with us when we were arrested. I had only the clothes I was wearing.

Daylight through slats in the siding was our only light. The train rolled along, then pulled to a halt from time to time, and stood for hours. Sometimes bombs fell nearby. Behavior broke down among our wretched numbers. Some panicked and became hysterical. Some cried. Some behaved like animals one to another. Some went into shock and withdrew completely. We had our own specially provided hell in those boxcars, which moved, then stopped, then moved again, but were not opened. After an unremembered number of days and nights the train came to its destination, for suddenly there was a great deal of noise and movement outside and the doors of our car were yanked open.

Blinking at the piercing light and barely able to move our joints, we were hustled out of the car by SS bullies who introduced us to the persuasive power of truncheons. "Raus! Raus! Raus! Raus!" they shouted as they laid into our backs with their clubs. During this frantic process people were also trying to collect their belongings.

"Leave your luggage alone. Leave it there. You'll get your luggage later," they ordered.

"Men over here! Women over there!"

Families tried to cling together, but were roughly pulled apart and lined up by sexes. Then the SS separated us further, ordering some of the men from the men's line and some of the women from theirs. I was ordered into a line of young men. Older men, perhaps 35 and older, were placed in another line with young boys below the age of 14 or 15. We did not yet know what this was all about. My line was marched into trucks and driven a few miles past crowded prisoner-of-war camps and what seemed like big chemical factories, belching smoke. We arrived at a tent camp where we were unloaded under the harsh proddings of Polish Jews who spoke only Yiddish. We Dutch Jews for the most part spoke little German or Yiddish and were at a loss to understand many of the commands barked at us. We felt completely isolated, unwanted aliens in a hostile landscape.

Those who had brought luggage never did see their luggage again. Before they had been packed onto the train, everyone had been persuaded to bring their valuables as well as their clothing and to prepare for a long stay. Once the Dutch Jews had left the train, the Nazis had confiscated everything.

We were assigned tent bunks, then lined up once more. We were ordered to strip, except for our shoes, and our clothing was immediately taken away. We were completely shaved, all of our major body hair, from head to crotch. Then consecutive identification numbers, in order of our arrival, were tattooed on our left forearms. Mine was 139829. Through this process we stood naked in the hot sun. At long last we were issued some old clothing of utterly indifferent fit and interrogated as to our professions and work skills prior to our being arrested. When asked what I did I told them I was a carpenter. Illogical as it might seem, I remembered reading in one of my texts that the basis of architecture was carpentry. If I was to work, I thought, I might as well start learning first hand about building.

That night, searching my mind for a few Yiddish words, I asked an "old timer" next to me what this place was and where it was. I learned that we had been transported to Silesia, a portion of southwest Poland, that we were in Buna, a sub-camp of Auschwitz, places that I had never heard of before. I also learned that we had been ordered to one of the fortunate lines when we disembarked from the boxcar. Everyone else had been gassed by then.

Rozetta Veerman (Max's mother), posing at Zandvoort when a young woman. Date of photo unknown.

1933 classroom picture: At lower left, Appie Klaverstyn (in glasses) sits beside Max R. Garcia, grinning and in dark tie, white shirt. Close friend Robbie Bleekrode sits directly behind Max in striped sleeveless pullover. Teacher Mevrouw van der Roest, in white-collared dress, stands among children near wall.

PART 3

THE CAMPS

Sippora and Max Rodriguez Garcia in a studio portrait taken on 7 August, 1935.

BUNA, 1943

I labored in the sub-camp of Buna for only a short time, perhaps a couple of weeks, helping to build a factory for I. G. Farben, a German munitions manufacturer. My fellow prisoners and I were ill-prepared for the harshness that was now our routine lot. Everyone who had some authority could and did beat us and badger us at their pleasure. There were the *Kapos* who were in charge of our individual laboring groups, or work details, as they were called, and who were answerable for the production of these groups. The *Kapos* were fellow prisoners who had been around for some time, earning their position by toughness and favors. The *Blockälteste*, similarly experienced prisoners, were in charge of each tent, and were helped by favored prisoners called *Stubenälteste*. The *Kapos* and the *Blockälteste* were often chosen from the Polish and German criminal or political elements, but there were experience-hardened Jews as well, bent on winning the daily game of survival. We ordinary prisoners were the *Häftlinge*. The SS guards and administrators exacted their due in various ways from the "prominent" prisoners, thus sparing themselves much of the unpleasant work of the daily prison routine. This system through which we were controlled I learned only slowly, however, and by many bitter lessons.

We slept on the straw-covered floor of immense tents. Each tent housed easily several hundred prisoners. We were awakened each morning before dawn and made to stand for long periods at roll call while our numbers and bodies were counted off in blocks, checked and rechecked. Each of us was assigned to an *Arbeitskommando*, or work force, to which we then reported for another line-up and roll call. Daily I marched off in my *Kommando*, accompanied by our *Kapos* and guards, to a factory which was some distance away from our camp on the other side of the military prisoner-of-war camps. I worked on the second floor of the Farben plant, carrying clay tiles back and forth. The work was heavy and was very hard on me. I had been accustomed to the robust diet of my homeland, even during the occupation, but in Buna I was hungry all the time. We *Häftlinge* received only a cup of tea, a bowl of soup, and a hunk of bread a day.

Lying in straw on our tent floor at night, we Dutch Jews whispered together, exchanging shocked stories about the incredible things each of us was experiencing. We asked one another if this inhuman regimen was to represent our last days on earth. Some were already growing weak, and many were heartsick with the knowledge of gassed loved ones or with wondering about the fate of dear ones. We tried to cheer one another with accounts of remembered family scenes but, often, choked back tears instead of finishing our stories. We described to one another the foods we missed most, the most memorable meals we had eaten, foods we planned to eat if we ever got away from this place.

I have mentioned that most of us Dutch Jews were at a loss to understand much of the German and Polish spoken by our guards. For this we suffered a great deal. One evening on the way back from the factory some words were hurled my way which I could not understand, and I was severely beaten by a *Kapo*. I broke down and cried. That night in my sleeping space I was still crying, utterly defeated, and too exhausted and hungry to sleep. That my father, mother, and sister were gone burst fully into my mind. Remembered scenes of our lives together ran through my head and were more than I could bear. And what did I have to look forward to? These madmen were going to work me until my last ounce of strength was gone. They wanted me to die. They couldn't wait for me to die. All around me, weakened, exhausted, dying men showed me what a little more time here would bring all of us to.

As I continued to mutter and sob out my despair, I heard a voice at my ear, a Polish voice. An older prisoner, probably in his late twenties, who was a tent mate, laid a hand on my shoulder. "Hey, young one," he tried first in Yiddish, then halting French, "don't cry. That won't help."

"But I can't help it. I am afraid to die," I got across in French. We began to talk to each other, switching languages, groping for words we might each understand. He asked me to tell him the story of my background, and I did as well as I could.

"That is a sad story, boy, but everyone here has a sad story to tell. So let me ask you this: do you want to survive this camp or die sometime soon like most of these poor bastards?"

"Of course, I want to live, but how in a place like this?"

"That's what I want to tell you, boy, and listen to me well. From now on never think of where you came from or about your family and friends. Think only of today and what you must do to stay ahead of your captors. Just figure you dropped out of the sky into this awful place. You have to survive. You have to live for the future. Forget all that has passed. Toughen up. Learn their games and outsmart them."

A heavy dose of philosophy these words were for me at the age of 19, but I thought about them a great deal and resolved to try to live by his advice. I wanted to hope. Without hope, I realized, I could not last many more days.

I concentrated on learning the meaning of the German and Polish phrases and epithets barked at us constantly, and made an effort to answer in their languages. I began to withdraw from many of the evening discussions about "the old days" among my fellow Dutch Jews. I paid attention to how things worked, who was controlling what, and what was happening in this prison. We *Häftlinge* knew by now about the electrified barbed-wire fencing around the camp—a high, menacing double fence, one about twelve feet inside the other. We had seen men throw themselves against the inside fence rather than experience another day. We knew now about the gas chambers and the crematoria in the Auschwitz camp complex. Instead of being gassed on our arrival as thousands were being gassed every week, we had been lucky enough to be assigned to a war factory slave force until we gave up our bodies to starvation and exhaustion. We did not see the gas chambers or the trainloads of people streaming into them, but we smelled the stench of the crematorium and saw its heavy, yellow-black smoke. The grapevine told us the rest.

I saw many men give up their will to live. I swore that I would never be one of them. I would try hard to live.

At the factory we worked as flunkies to civilians, along with some British and French prisoners-of-war. These were enlisted men who, according to the Geneva Convention, could be forced to work. The Convention was honored in the matter of their officers, who were protected from such labor. In the hope of cadging a bite to eat or a cigarette, I decided one day to try to talk to a French soldier working beside me. Hearing me, a *Kapo* put a stripe across my back with his hose, and ordered me not to try to talk with the prisoners-of-war. On the way back to the factory the next day, however, this same *Kapo* moved next to me to whisper: "Hey, you! Do you like to talk with those Frenchmen? Well, now, I'll let you have one little talk today if you'll promise to get me some cigarettes."

"I'll try," I muttered in German, surprised, frightened, hopeful. I managed to cadge three cigarettes from my French work companion, which I took to the *Kapo* and was rewarded with one for myself. From then on the *Kapo* counted on me at the factory. I bummed cigarettes and small handouts of food, first with my French, then trying my English. All booty was given over to the sharp-eyed *Kapo*, who paid me always with a small share.

AUSCHWITZ, 1943

In the process of setting down a heavy load at the factory one day, I crushed my left middle finger. I wrapped it up and tried to forget it but in a matter of days a painful abscess developed. I applied for and received permission to visit the first-aid station. The doctor took a look at my infection, then ordered me for treatment to the Auschwitz Main Camp hospital. Here I was lucky for had I not still been a fairly new prisoner, still comparatively strong and well fleshed out, they would not have bothered to keep me alive. Thus, in late July of 1943, I was transferred to the main hospital in Auschwitz, where I was placed in a ward of prisoners with communicable diseases. The finger was treated, I was allowed to rest, and the infection subsided. Discharged, I was not sent back to Buna but assigned to a laboring *Kommando* within the Auschwitz camp. This was another typical slave-laboring detail requiring us to stoop, lift, fetch, and carry.

I was assigned to an enormous brick barracks building, one of streets of similar two-story buildings, some with basement punishment cells. We slept in bunks stacked four high in a forest of bunks which were reached by means of a central and several secondary corridors. The bunks were wooden, filled with straw, and covered with a dirty piece of blanket.

Very few Dutch Jews were transferred out of Buna into the main camp. Along with a few Dutch Jews there was a scattering of Dutch gentiles, but in my barracks none were nearby. I was surrounded mostly by Poles and Germans. Life in our barracks was primitive. Arguments, pushing, and shoving were routine.

"You stole the bread I was hiding," one prisoner would accuse another.

"No, I did not steal your bread," the other would answer.

"I was in line first!"

"No, I was here first and you know it!"

Fighting sometimes broke out at the lunch-time soup line at the work site over places. Cries of "Stir the soup before you serve me!" were often heard from prisoners who knew that unless the soup was stirred the solids would settle to the bottom.

At night in the barracks no one complained that we were compelled to turn in early, but there were complaints, socks, and kicks over too much turning on another's part, or constant snores, coughs, or noises.

Dim barracks lights were kept on all through the night, but it was not unusual to have them flicker out from time to time. We knew than that some desperate prisoner had gone out and thrown himself on the electric wires, thereby shorting out the electrical system. In the morning we would turn out on the *Appellplatz* to see the burned up remains of a former prisoner hanging there on the fence. It was not until all *Kommandos* marched off to work that the guards turned off the electric wiring and had the remains of the victim scraped from the fence and sent over to the crematorium.

In the early days of my arrival at Auschwitz before I was assigned to a permanent *Arbeitskommando*, I served in a clean-up detail that entered the twelve-foot corridor between the electric fences each morning after the electricity was turned off. Followed by gun-toting guards, we picked up litter that had blown into the area. I managed to hide in my clothing a few usable scraps of paper and cloth.

After I was admitted to the main prison, the makeshift clothing I had been issued in Buna was replaced by a grey and blue striped uniform. Only my still serviceable leather shoes were still on my feet. We had lightweight clothing for summer, heavier for winter, all of it striped— our sole possessions except for a tin soup tray and spoon. As part of our uniforms we also wore a matching striped cap. The cap was required daytime wear, and it had to be removed whenever an SS guard passed by. As a new prisoner I was sickened to witness the stamping and kicking senseless of a prisoner who forgot to remove his cap when an SS guard walked by.

My head was again shaved and a two-inch-wide stripe of hair was left standing in the center. The entire prison population wore that haircut, except for some "elite" criminal and political prisoners who had served in the camps for so many years that they were permitted to cut their hair in the style of the SS guards. Many months later our center stripe cut was reversed. The hair was then allowed to grow out about a half-inch over our skulls, and a two-inch-wide stripe was mowed down the center.

My uniform bore an insignia patch, a red and yellow Star of David identifying me as a Jew. As I remember, the red triangle of the star was up, the yellow down. My prison number, the same one tattooed on my forearm, was printed to the side of the insignia, which was worn on the upper left side of the shirt and the right trouser leg of the pants. The prisoners displayed a variety of insignia patches. Except for the Jews, these were in the form of triangles: Green for "criminals" (mostly German), red for "politicals" (enemies of the state of many nationalities), purple for Jehovah's Witnesses. There were black triangles, yellow, and others, the designations for which I do not remember.

On a typical Auschwitz day, as at Buna, we were awakened at 5:30 AM with loud cries of "Aufstehen!" "Aufstehen!" as the barracks lights were turned up. We lined up at the latrines, then the water tap to splash cold water over our faces before heading into the early morning air to line up again for our ration of what was called "tea." At least it was hot. We downed the tea with a hunk of bread which we had learned to save from our bread ration of the night before. At times, there was a little margarine or salami or ersatz cheese which we spread on the bread with a spoon filed down on one edge to use as a knife. At that hour we were usually cold, summer or winter, and the food was inadequate to take the chill from our bodies. I had learned to divide my nightly ration of bread into three hunks. One piece I ate at night when it was doled out, one piece in the morning with tea. At mid-morning on the job site when I felt faint from lack of food, I would head off into the stinking latrine to eat my third portion of bread in secret, ignoring the reeking filth and the flies. I chose to eat and to hold onto life.

At 6 AM a bell sounded to summon us for line-up outside our barracks. We found our places and started counting off by fives. Always we grouped in units of five, blocks of twenty, groups of one hundred. When the long chore of counting and rechecking was completed, we were permitted to return to our barracks for a half-hour, supposedly to clean them. What we were doing mainly, those of us who had the strength, was attempting to clean ourselves. Our bodies were crawling with lice, and we worked frantically to keep their numbers down. We would take extra time to wash ourselves at the cold water tap, take our clothes off to shake them out, then sit like monkeys picking lice from our bodies and out of the seams of our garments. As I have mentioned we wore the same clothes at all times. Our work clothes by day were our extra blanket at night. Our prison stripes were never washed. When we washed our bodies, we used whatever pieces of cloth for toweling we could find and hide away so that we would not have to go out with wet clothing.

We were vigilant to pick up any scraps of paper or cloth, even leaves, not only to wrap around our feet or wear under our shirts for warmth, but to use for cleaning ourselves after bowel movements. We jealously guarded and washed scraps of material that could serve as toweling.

The bell would sound again and we would break for the *Appellplatz* where the prisoners lined up daily with their *Arbeitskommando*, or work detail. The camp resembled a small city. Streets of enormous barracks fed into the main street which led to the *Appellplatz*. Early morning found the entire prison population turned out here in ranks according to their *Arbeitskommando*. The process of marching out the *Kommandos* was not unlike the assembling of a civic parade. Curious as it may seem, the SS provided a marching band, composed of recruited prisoners, to tootle us out of the gate each morning. The band *Kommando* assembled along with the rest of us, and, when we were all present and accounted for, struck up martial tunes as we began our orderly cadenced march through the formal, wrought-iron entry gate, each *Kommando* in its proper order.

As our group marched through the gate, we fetched our caps off our heads to the order, "Mutzen ab!" We marched five abreast in rows usually of twenty, depending on the size of the *Arbeitskommando*. Some were five-hundred strong. A few were composed of no more than twelve men. Each group had its *Kapo* and assistant *Kapo*. Once beyond the gate SS guards fell in on either side and behind us. As each *Kommando* veered off in the direction of its assigned work, prisoners dropped their military cadence; our posture slumped in favor of an exhausted shuffle toward our job sites. We worked at bending, lifting, carrying from about 7:30 AM until noon. Our guards prodded us often to work faster, and beat any of us soundly who were caught pausing to rest. At midday soup kettles were brought to the site and we were lined up to hold out our bowls for our daily ration of thin soup. This was our main meal for the day. To eat was to feel only slightly fueled. We no longer felt hunger pains but we were glassy-eyed with the effort of forcing our ebbing energy. A half an hour later we crawled back to work and labored until 4:30 PM when the clean-up process began. By 5 PM, we were straggling back to the camp in rough formation, our strength utterly used up.

The process of return was a little less demanding than the morning routine in that we could enter the camp in the order of our arrival. At the gates we were greeted once more with musical fanfare. After the first few days we no longer looked up as we entered to read the mocking words, "*Arbeit Macht Frei*" (Work Gives Freedom), spelled out in wrought iron on the entrance side of the gate's iron archway. If an SS guard became suspicious that any prisoner might be concealing something he had *organisiert* outside the camp, that prisoner was singled out for a body search. So went our routine six days a week.

Sunday was a day off and we could rest. Food rations were cut down on Sundays, but I learned it was a good day to scavenge for needed items and to make contacts among the privileged in the hope of being given a job or errand that paid off in food.

The soles of my leather shoes gradually disappeared from my feet, and I was issued a pair of rough wooden clogs. Fortunately, I knew how to keep my feet warm in clogs by wrapping them, for I had had plenty of practice in Holland during the lean years. I looked about me constantly on the work site and in the camp for scraps of paper or rags with which to keep my feet warm and dry. The protection of my feet I was learning and observing was the key to my survival. I saw the feet and ankles of many a prisoner swell up with malnutrition, and observed that death generally followed. I saw the wet and frozen toes of some of my fellow prisoners rot from gangrene, and again, death followed naturally, or was given a helping hand. Any injury, infection, or circulation defect in the lower extremities could be fatal. Taking good care of my feet became an obsession. I guarded them as well as possible as I worked, and watched where I put them down. No matter how tired or sick I might feel, I washed and dried my feet attentively each day.

Once every few months the camp administration surprised us with a shower and delousing process for the whole barracks at one time. The order, without fail, came at night. "Hey, you bastards, strip and head for the bathhouse. Move!" "Raus! Raus!" Ordered out a floor at a time, we started running in line through the cold night air, hastened along by lashes to our backs and legs from the hoses of the *Kapos* and the SS. At the bathhouse we were driven through a battery of cold-water showers where we washed ourselves as quickly as possible with a small piece of crude soap. At the end of the shower room we were halted before other prisoners armed with rough-bristled brushes which they filled with a strong delousing solution and applied vigorously to our heads, armpits, and crotches. We dashed naked back into the now freezing night air and to our bunks. There we tried to dry ourselves, but spent the rest of the night shivering, losing the battle to regain our lost bodily warmth. Indeed, we found that as malnutrition took its toll, we were less and less able to cope with extremes of heat and cold.

The term for a dying man among the *Häftlinge* was "*Muselmänn*," and *Muselmänner*, being poor workers, were not kept around long. We grew accustomed to seeing members of the *Totenkommando* pulling open carts filled with Musselmanner towards the gas chambers. The *Muselmanner* were stripped of their shirts and bore their prison identity numbers in bold stenciling across their bare chests. Some moaned, some cried out for help, some kept their silence, some prayed with others as they were slowly pulled to their doom. We *Häftlinge* soon learned to look away when we heard these death carts coming.

After a number of weeks of work in my assigned put-down-pick-up detail, my number was called out during one of the morning count downs. This was a dangerous matter, to have my number called out like that, and my heart began pounding with fright. I reported to the location ordered and learned, to my immense relief, that I had been reassigned to another work detail. I could hardly believe my good fortune to be told I was to report to the carpentry *Kommando*. By now, however, the main cause of my happiness was that I was going to work inside. It was already September, and winter would not be long in coming. The card noting my trade had evidently made its way through channels from Buna.

I started my job in high spirits though I had never done any work like it before. All prisoners in the *Kommando* presumably were carpenters. I watched them and did what they did in the midst of the heavy and sharp-bladed machinery of our plant: rabbeters, sanders, planers, saws. I shoved boards through a planing machine to another man who picked them up. Together we stacked them. The work was hard but at least I was doing something I found interesting. Above all, it was pleasant to be indoors as the fall wind and rain blew wildly across the camp area. There were no other Dutch prisoners in the carpentry *Kommando*. My German and Polish were improving daily. All other languages, I had come to realize, had no value. They were useful only for social communication. They did not help a man survive. For instance, all prison numbers were called out in German or Polish each morning. Woe to the prisoner who did not comprehend an order directly addressed to him.

Many of the *Kapos* were Polish and, hating the Germans, did not like German to be spoken to them. The SS used only German. Both the Poles and the Germans were extremely anti-Semitic. I determined to learn both languages well to try to overcome some of the overwhelming odds against me as a Jew. If you could converse with your enemy, I figured, there was the possibility of getting through to him as a human being, even of getting one of those extra jobs that contributed to survival.

Eventually, I managed to do just that. I was assigned to help bring the tea to the barracks early in the morning and, on Sundays, the soup. This meant that I had to get up much earlier than the others and give up precious resting time on Sunday, but to get a little extra tea or soup that way was worth it. I would scrape out the empty wooden soup bucket with my fingers. By occasionally winning the chore of shining the shoes of *Kapos* or *Blockälteste* I could get a piece of bread. Thus I traded my extra labor for food, and developed my skills at *Organisierung,* which meant the gathering in of things by any means available for one's personal needs. It did not mean stealing from other needy prisoners.

I held my ground in the carpentry shop. If I was not an efficient worker, my defects did not stand out. None of us were efficient. The Nazis understood that if they got a fifty-percent effort from their prisoners they were doing well. The heavy output of the plant came from paid civilian employees under whom we worked. Our *Kapos* were responsible for providing a certain quota of prisoners per day and seeing that they produced a modicum of work. If too many prisoners began reporting sick, the *Kapos* would crack down and beat any man who had reported sick when he returned to work. We had to weigh these factors, and most of us did not report to the hospital without good reason.

AUSCHWITZ, 1944

By midwinter, probably January, 1944, I became acquainted with a new member of the band *Kommando*. He was a tall Jewish boy from Amsterdam who had recently been pulled from labor in a coal-mining sub-camp to play in the band in the main camp. He was the only prisoner I allowed myself to drop my guard with and to befriend during this period when we worked in daily contact with one another. I can see his face and long, angular body to this day, but his name is lost to my memory. When he turned up in the band *Kommando* I was pleased to encounter a spirited fellow Mokummer; and, though he was several years older than I, we became friends.

Evenings and mornings we gabbed together in Dutch, sotto voce. Secretly we laughed together over his story of how he had landed in the Auschwitz band *Kommando*. He had been a professional musician, a trumpet player, in Amsterdam until he was rounded up and transported to Silesia as part of a Jewish slave-laboring force for Nazi coal mines. While he was working there his SS guards heard that he had once been a musician and began to make gibes about the trumpet-playing miner. One evening close to Christmas, after the SS had been drinking heavily, they sent for him and presented him with an old trumpet that one of them had been able to *organisier*. "Play it for us," they ordered. "Play *Silent Night*, Jew. Surely if you are a musician you know it well."

He described the ludicrous scene in which his drunken guards demanded of their Jewish prisoner that he play

Silent Night for them. My friend said he was anxious about the kind of shape the instrument might be in, and he knew very well that his lip was poor from lack of practice. Nevertheless, he raised the trumpet to his lips and managed to get through the Christmas carol. In their maudlin state the SS guards thought the performance was wonderful. From then on my friend was ordered to play a great deal, and he discovered that the trumpet was a miraculous tool for gaining extra food and favors. His reputation developed with his performances. Then, suddenly, he was ordered transferred to Auschwitz Main to the band *Kommando*.

He played mornings and afternoons at the gate, and occasionally for SS private parties or socials at night. The band *Kommando* was soft duty. The musicians stayed in the camp all day doing a few odd jobs. Extra rations easily came their way because music was an important luxury in such a depressing environment. My friend carried his trumpet with him wherever he went, a proud symbol of his special status.

He introduced me to one or two other Dutch musicians in the band, and we all became companionable. Here were some countrymen with some morale left to them. I sought them out. The humor and high spirits we encouraged in one another's company were good medicine. We discovered the balm of laughter. What a joke our predicament was! We all laughed. We understood one another. One of the *Blockälteste* was a former boxing champion from Holland. He allowed us to gather in his office bedroom to talk and to vie with one another for favors. As a *Blockälteste*, he was in charge of a barracks block housing somewhere between 2,000 and 3,000 inmates. A cadre of *Stubenälteste* of his choosing helped with the many housekeeping and organizatioanl details of the block, including supplies and record-keeping. Sometimes some of us were recruited to do this or that extra chore. We took particular interest in the details of food distribution for the block. If an inmate died, that day there would be an extra ration of bread to hand out as a favor for work performed. No one shed a tear or felt a pang of guilt over such bonuses.

My trumpet-playing friend and I visited often in the *Blockälteste's* office, talking of the Amsterdam we once called home, he of his various entertainment adventures, I of my own exploits. My stories were those of a family boy while his, impressively, were those of a man-about-town. Since he talked of music I began to recall my own part in various family entertainments that we children had staged from time to time. I used to sing French, German, and Dutch popular songs at family gatherings. I had been encouraged to believe I had a good voice, and an indulgent audience watched my imitations of Maurice Chevalier, even to the straw hat and cane, and Charles Trenet, another popular French singer. Laughing over our reminiscences, we each tried out some of our old routines on our friends.

They cheered and an idea dawned among us. Why not try some kind of show for the prisoners with popular musical numbers and jokes? It could be like a cabaret, less the refreshments and the price of admission. The payoff would be in the lifting of spirits, not only our fellow prisoners' but ours in putting together an entertainment. Our group became quite excited about the idea, including the *Blockälteste,* who agreed to approach the camp authorities in our behalf.

At first the SS would not hear of it. We were not to play jazz music such as my friend had suggested. That was decadent and *verboten*. What about the idea in general, we asked. Could we play for the prisoners, and, if so, what? After many discussions they gave us a tentative approval to plan a preview performance for the authorities. We could play some German cabaret music as well as some officially approved tunes. A comedy routine that steered clear of political satire could be tried.

We were not particularly pleased with the limited repertoire we settled for, but it was better than nothing, and we were ready to do anything just to go, go, go. Energy flowed through us as we planned our new endeavor. Except for occasional bonuses of extra bread for chores performed, I ate the rations of the *Häftlinge;* yet I looked forward to putting in night rehearsal time with my musician friends after a day's work in the carpentry shop. We rehearsed until we were satisfied that we had put together a pretty good act, then invited the whole SS upper echelon for an exclusive preview.

The show went over beyond our wildest expectations. I was not the leader of the group, but because I could sing a little, tell jokes, and ad-lib to audience remarks, I played the "master of ceremonies" while others played instruments. We did German movie tunes, slapstick, and common street jokes, French songs, and some popular tunes with jazz overtones. The SS men clapped and roared with laughter. After the show, they gave their approval for our doing a Sunday cabaret for the prisoners. We were elated. There was something in it for us besides the love of entertaining, and we knew it. We were callously selfish in looking forward to the favored treatment and the little extras that would come our way because of the SS approval of our enterprise.

The prisoners laughed and applauded the cabaret, and we genuinely enjoyed entertaining them. Because of our success, we were permitted to hold regular Sunday performances in one of the blocks. Prisoners could come and go as they pleased, and we always drew a good audience.

Weekdays my work routine in the carpentry *Kommando* did not change until one morning—it must have been early March—when my number was once more called out for special report. What now? Alarmed, I reported in, as directed. To my amazement I had been reassigned to the roofing *Kommando.* Roofing? I was horrified. Not only did I not want outside work, but roofs were just not my choice, what with the chance of falling off.

The permanent work force at Auschtwitz Main had what they called an "appeals line," where one could express grievances. I wasted no time hiking over to stand in it. At the front of the line an SS officer listened to prisoners' complaints and made rulings on them then and there. When my turn came to present my case I explained that I had been performing a useful job in the carpentry shop, that my *Kapo* would verify that I was doing good work, that I had never done roofing work and, therefore, my talents would be wasted.

The officer heard me out, then stated, "Request denied. Next!" I could not believe that he had understood me correctly, and, determined to enunciate my German more clearly, I returned to the back of the line. When I stood before the officer once more I began to tell him that I did not think he had understood my appeal. His fist came forward into my face like an unexpected battering ram. I awoke in my barracks bunk. A couple of friends were standing over me telling me what an idiot I had been to try to argue with the Appeals SS. They had seen me go down and had dragged me away fast before the officer could think about what should be done with me.

Fellow prisoners saved me from my foolishness, and I turned up in a hurry at the roofing *Kommando*. Our work consisted of repairing roofs, most of which were composed of clay tile. Cold winds and rain blew against our backs as we worked, but we rejoiced as the sun gained strength. On sunny days we took our shirts off and let the rays of the sun flow through our bodies.

We were sent quite often to a sub-camp called Birkenau to repair the tile roofs of brick or wooden barrack buildings. This was the women's camp, but it was also the known location of the gas chambers and crematoria. Even from the rooftops on which we worked we were not in a position to observe operations in these death-dealing buildings. We did not know which building housed the gas chambers, but smoke and stench made the crematoria unmistakable. I preferred to look at the women in the courtyards below. This interest was not consciously sexual —people who are starving have little sexual appetite. I had heard that many of these women were Dutch, and I longed to communicate. Eventually I wrote a note in Dutch on a paper scrap with a pencil stub I had *organisiert*. I rolled the note in a ball and threw it down among a group of women when the eyes of the guards were turned away. Soon word was passed back to me to look in a certain place in the latrine the next day before our *Kommando* returned to the main camp. I took their news back to the main camp. The Dutch men were very interested and wanted as much news as I could bring and pass around. We had a strong nucleus of Dutch entertainers in our cabaret, and, inevitably, it occurred to us to ask permission to take our cabaret over to Birkenau for a single Sunday to entertain the women. Again, the SS stalled and debated, but we persisted and were eventually granted the permission we sought with a strict warning that there be no attempt at personal communication.

Thus, one summer Sunday we brought together our instruments and a few props for transportation over to Birkenau. In the camps, all transportation of prisoners' equipment and supplies was accomplished by flatbed carts fitted with horse shafts and rolled by wooden wheels, large ones in back, smaller ones in front. Instead of horses, prisoners manned the shafts while other prisoners pushed at the sides and the back. The musicians and players of our cabaret, steering a flatbed cart full of instruments and equipment, pushed and sweated our way out of the gates of our camp, then staggered and rolled, under guard, the awkward distance to Birkenau, a walk for us of little less than an hour.

Women jammed the barracks hall in which we performed. Some peered in through the windows. As so many of the performers were Dutch and as I was the master of ceremonies, we used many Dutch songs and old comic routines. As we had hoped, we were rewarded with an enthusiastic response from the Dutch women. In fact, the enthusiasm of the entire audience was wildly expressed. Notes reached our hands and stealthy whispers reached our ears through the hubbub. These cheering women bombarded us with pathetic pleas: Did we know if a husband, so and so, was still alive? Had we seen so and so? Did we have news of a son, husband, or other relative? What were our names? Would we please carry this note to so and so. How could we stay in touch? Would we come back?

Auschwitz, 1944

Midway through the performance, this underlying but unvoiced scream to us of grief and despair reached a crescendo. We did not know how to cope with these women. Silent and depressed after the show, we dragged our cartload of equipment back to the main camp. We could not put in words how we felt, and did not try. Probably the Dutch cabaret musicians felt as defeated as I did. The experience had been unsettling. We had been made to realize just how ineffectual we were before the women's reminders of our real problems. The Dutch women had looked right through our cabaret game; in fact, had played it well themselves. But they were expecting something more from us by way of help. We had to admit to ourselves that we were no longer men with the power to help them. We were less than men. We were survivors.

Nevertheless, as a roofer working regularly at Birkenau, I continued to function as a messenger for the Dutch women. We were playing a dangerous game, but scraps of information between the camps continued. I picked up notes at designated spots, memorized them, then destroyed them. We all became wiser but sadder. We exchanged information on who was living and who was dead. The survival statistics did not make comforting news. From what I can now recollect and from what knowledge I had then, there were probably no more than ten men from our Amsterdam transport (which may have numbered 1,000 people) who survived Auschwitz with me. I do not know about the women.

As weeks passed, the cabaret lost its novelty as a way to spend our extra energy and time. The prisoners had become thoroughly familiar with our routines; and so, by mutual agreement, we disbanded.

At our work on the rooftops one day, my fellow workers and I were halted from our labors by the sounding of a general alarm, the signal to the main camp and all sub-camps that there had been an escape. We were called down for a line-up of our *Kommando*. The *Kapo* took pains to count us over carefully. We stood in our places for a long period of time until the winnowing process through all the *Kommandos* turned up the missing men. Later we heard that the men hunted had been found and executed. The block from which they came had been subjected to beatings and special brutalities for allowing the escape to occur. I did not know the details for it was not our block, but the grapevine quickly passed around the news. I was amazed at the courage of these men who tried to escape because the chances seemed so little possible. One barbed-wire-surrounded camp was placed right next to another so that to get through one fence meant only to be enclosed in a new cage. If a prisoner managed the impossible and broke through all fenced compounds—or, more likely, escaped from a labor detail outside the camp gates—he would have found himself free in anti-Semitic Poland where help would have been hard to find.

The most vivid escape attempt in my memory concerned six prisoners who were caught after a long search. Mornings and evenings over a few days' time we then observed the construction of three gallows in front of the kitchen building to one side of the *Appellplatz*. One evening when construction was completed, we were ordered to mass in the *Appellplatz,* an unusual occurrence. Six Polish political prisoners were marched out before us, hands tied behind their backs. They were brought to a halt before the gallows, and suddenly these brave men shouted, "Down with Hitler! Down with Germany! Long live the Allies!" The SS guard descended on them, yanked their trousers down and lashed their buttocks with truncheons, leaning into the blows, delivering fourteen strokes in all. They hung them then, one by one, before our eyes.

I had counted the blows, I could not help it, but I had tried to avoid watching this spectacle closely. I think many of us looked down or to the right or left as much as we dared. We prisoners had become resigned to watching people die around us or throwing themselves against the electric fences. We did not like it but we expected it at any time. Death was like a fellow prisoner who walked alongside, behind, or in front of us. We were so aware of his presence among us that we hardly noticed him. Yet to be forced to witness the brutal lashing and hanging of some of our number, a few men who had been particularly brave, was hard for us to have to stomach. Death was flaunting his terrible power before our reluctant eyes. We were frightened and ashamed to have had to serve as witnesses.

As cold spring rains whipped us while we worked atop roofs, I developed a cold which gradually grew worse. When I could no longer make work call, I was given permission to go to the hospital. The inmate doctor who examined me told me I had pnuemonia. All prisoners, incidentally, were examined and treated by doctors who were themselves prisoners, wearing their insignia and camp numbers on their hospital coats. The examining doctor ordered me to remove my shirt and bend over the back of a chair, placing my hands on the seat. When my back was taut, he inserted a long needle into one lung and pulled out some fluid into his syringe. I was assigned a bunk in a hospital ward, and the needle sucking process was repeated daily until the fluid stopped collecting. The bed rest was very welcome. I slept for hours at a time. We were fed the same rations as the working *Häftlinge*.

I began to feel well enough to get up and walk about. I walked frequently past our ward windows, staring surreptitiously at the women's barracks of the hospital, which our ward faced. I had heard that about eighty percent of the women there were Dutch and that the SS were said to be performing some dubious experiments on them, the exact nature of which was unknown. Whenever I was not in danger of being observed by the *Stubenälteste*, I watched their barracks window and tried to catch the eye of one or another of the women. Since their windows were no more than thirty feet away from ours, some of us gradually began to establish some signals of recognition, then to communicate in Dutch by lip-reading. Many of these women, I learned, were being used for experiments in sterilization and artificial insemination. They learned from me about my pnuemonia, and then, to my surprise, managed to smuggle over to me a small supply of calcium tablets. They sent some more at intervals, and I began to feel stronger. Yet, just short of full recovery I succumbed to another bout of pneumonia. Once more I was bedridden, and the dreadful needle process was started again. Throughout a second recovery period my compassionate women friends continued to supply me with calcium tablets, which they must have *organisiert* from their hospital.

On sporadic occasions the SS doctors ordered an inspection routine in the ward. This consisted of directing all the patients on the ward to line up, naked, at one end of the room before an SS doctor who, sitting in his chair and looking us over one by one, decided on the spot who was worth keeping and who was not. A left or right jerk of his thumb sent each of us off either to the gas chamber or back to bed for further recuperation. By now, at the age of 20, I knew my captors well. When my turn before the doctor came I would step briskly forward and click the barely covered bones of my heels together so that the crack could be distinctly heard. I would stand smartly at attention, muscles taut. Never mind that I was skinny and run down. Every one of us was skinny and run down. Never mind that I was weak and faint and scared, literally, to death. Every one of us felt that way.

Week after week the doctor signaled me back to my hospital bunk. I would return on unsure legs, my mouth dry, my blood racing. Climbing back into my clothes I would find that I was trembling all over. At the same time I felt giddy with triumph, and preferred to dwell on my personal euphoria rather than the plight of my fellow ward mates who were soon to perish. I would signal my women friends about my survival of a selection and they would smile and make victory signs They were my rooting team, cheering me as I signaled my survival of selection after selection. In the weeks of my hospitalization, I went through this process several times. Each time I returned to my bunk, heady with personal triumph. They were not going to get Max Garcia, not that way.

As for the doomed patients who were designated to be gassed, they were kept around the ward for a day or two until orders for their transportation to the gas chambers could be effected. When the SS turned up to herd them into a waiting truck, we remaining patients experienced the guilty pleasure of a reduced ward population. Some of us could get a better blanket now or change to a better bunk with better straw and fewer lumps. There were also lighter cleanup duties for the rest of us as the critically ill disappeared from our ranks. An ambulatory patient like myself helped with the scrubbing of the floors, general maintenance, and care of the more helpless patients. Many of us hustled to do the extra work necessary to come into the good graces of the *Stubenälteste*, who controlled our food supply. Every death on the ward meant extra rations, at least for that day. We vied with one another to be rewarded with an additional hunk of bread or bowl of soup.

There was an underground song that went around among the prisoners, which started:

"Auschwitz, Auschwitz
I cannot forget you
As long as I remain alive..."

It ended:

"...and if I survive Auschwitz
I will never die again."

THE PAKETSTELLE KOMMANDO 1944

After eight weeks I was discharged from the hospital as cured of pneumonia, and, because I had been out of circulation for so long, I was assigned to new barracks and a new bunk. The very night of my return I was awakened by an excruciating pain in the abdomen. I am able to recall that it was a Thursday night because of the ordeal that followed. Wave after wave of nauseating pain convulsed me and nothing I tried relieved it. I could not lie down, or sit up, or stand up without great pain. Straightening my backbone was the least bearable position so I assumed a doubled over posture whether walking or lying. I felt a constant urge to relieve myself but could not do so.

In the morning I was to report for reassignment to a work detail. Instead, I was compelled to report once more to the clinic. This time, I figured, my fate had caught up with me. I could hardly walk, much less work. At the clinic the doctor checked me over, then sent me back to my bunk for the day. My condition did not improve. The next morning the doctor told me to return to my bunk and to stay there through the Saturday workday and through Sunday. He said he expected I would be sufficiently recuperated to report for work on Monday. Three more miserable days went by. Fevered, in terrible pain, I writhed on my bunk, then paced about doubled over. Each passing hour seemed like many. On Monday morning I slowly dragged my doubled-over, old-man's body toward the clinic. It was as if I could see myself through a window, heading for my own destruction but powerless to care.

This time, after the doctor examined me, he stepped to his desk and made a telephone call. "I have a Jew here with a 4½ day-old acute appendicitis, herr Doktor... Yes, it is amazing... Very well, sir, Goodbye."

The doctor returned to my side to tell me that I was to be operated on. He wrote out orders for me to take over to the surgical unit, and before I could recover from my astonishment, I was on my way. I walked to the surgical hospital where a staff member received my note, then assigned me a bunk in which to wait. The wait seemed long before I was escorted into an operating room and assisted onto the table. The inmate doctor who had examined me at the clinic entered and began directing me. He was to be my surgeon. He told me to sit forward with my arms around my knees and to tighten up my back. I did so. In so much pain I did not care much what

The Paketstelle Kommando, 1944

was next, I felt a needle entering my spine. Immediately the area froze, and, as the pain receded, I was turned around and laid out flat upon the table. My body was covered with sheets. A little screen was placed before my face by an orderly who stood at my head. I could see mirrored images in the shiny metal lamp above the operating table. An SS doctor entered. I could see his uniform pants and boots as he walked past my head. I felt a little zip like a nail sliding across my belly. Through the metallic reflection of the lamp I could see the inmate surgeon receive some instruments and bend over my body to do his work. The SS doctor looked on. The operation looked and felt very remote. Then the surgeon began to stitch the incision, and, as he did so, the SS doctor walked wordless from the room.

I was to learn later through the hospital grapevine that the only reason I had been operated on was that the SS doctor who came in to watch was a young surgeon who had never seen an operation on an acute appendicitis ready to burst, and he wished to have that experience. According to what I was able to learn in my prison years at Auschwitz, I was the only Jew to receive an operation there. Such was one quirk of my survival.

Orderlies placed me on a gurney and trundled me to the recuperation ward next to the operating room. I was half-lifted, half-tossed into a lower bunk. Here the bunks were only two, not four, tiers high. With returning awareness I was grateful for the extra room. I lay in straw with straw dust from the bunk over me falling freely. I began to shiver from the shock of the operation. I was so cold that I slept for only moments at a time. My teeth clattered as my sleepless body was wracked with uncontrollable shaking. Finally, I screamed out. An orderly brought me an extra blanket. It was thin and of not much help, but his considerate act helped calm me.

My body did not begin to generate warmth again until almost two days had passed. There was no medication, but we did receive better food rations in the surgical unit. In addition to the usual daily portions, there was a bowl of breakfast gruel each morning. I was expected to care for my throbbing wound by myself. Other patients gave me instructions. But the operated area did not drain properly and it quickly developed pus. After a few days, the doctor had me walk over to yet another hospital. There on another operating table, I was opened up again and the abscessed wound cleaned out and repaired.

I was installed in another recovery ward where, once more, the bunks were the typical four high, the cases of this ward being considered less serious than those of my first postoperative ward. The ward stank from many putrid open wounds like mine. Clean cotton and bandages were scarce. Pus ran freely from our wounds as we tried to clean and drain them ourselves. Filthy swabs and rags wound up on the floor where we would slip on them when we left the bunks to use the latrines and to wash ourselves. I gave my wound close attention, learning to clean and care for it with no aids other than water and rags which could hardly pass muster as clean.

Because of the stench of our various festering openings, the windows were kept open. We could lay on our bunks and watch the changing skies above the high charged-wire fence not far beyond the building. It was during my stay in this ward that I watched the destruction of the gypsies in the compound on the other side of the fence outside our window. Male and female gypsies, rounded up and thrown together in this compound like so many chickens in a coop, could be seen sitting about or promenading dejectedly in groups. One day I was attracted to the window by shouts and scuffling in the gypsy camp. Men and women were grappling with guards, trying to overpower them, but more rifle-bearing guards appeared. Shots echoed through the air and some of the gypsies fell dead. The compound quieted down again, but not long afterwards the gypsies were all lined up and led out of the compound, not to return.

The area of my incision gradually stopped draining, and after four weeks or so I was discharged as healed. Sensitive skin now covered a ragged wound in my right lower abdomen, and to this day the operation site looks like a butcher's battlefield. As appendicitis scars go, mine may

The Paketstelle Kommando, 1944

be an eyesore, but for me it is almost a badge of pride, for I know that without it I would have been ashes by the time Auschwitz was liberated.

After a stay of about three months in what must have been one of the longest consecutive hospitalizations on record in the prison, I was released to new barracks and ordered to report for work assignment the next morning. The weather was warm but summer was giving way to fall, and over a year had gone by since my arrival in the camp. The numbers on my fellow prisoners' arms read considerably higher than mine. The number tattooed on my arm, 139829, compared with the far higher ones on other arms, singled me out as a living relic, an unusual specimen among *Häftlinge*.

Morning lineup found me standing with others at the assignment area in front of the kitchen, waiting orders from the *Arbeitskapo*, a prisoner in charge of assigning men to the various *Kommandos* of the camp. The *Arbeitskapo* was a highly privileged prisoner, a fact we all knew but which was emphasized by the neatness of his appearance and the excellent condition of his clothing. His prison stripes actually looked tailor-made. His shoes were of leather.

"Well, where have you been?" he asked me, glancing at the number on my jacket. "In the hospital," I replied. "There are damn few of you left with a number as low as yours," he said. I nodded, and the *Arbeitskapo* continued, "Seems to me anybody who can survive as long as you deserves a break." He wrote out a work-assignment note and handed it to me. *"Melde Dich an Paketstelle"* was what I read on the paper. (Report to the package agency.) Wonderful! Indoor work again. I could have used a little sunlight at that point, but when I thought of the freezing Silesian winter ahead of us, I felt lucky. However, having never received a parcel at the camp, I knew nothing about the operations of the *Paketstelle*, or post office, as we called it, even though only packages were handled there.

It was but a few steps to the post office from the assignment area where I stood. I entered, reported to the

Kapo, and looked around. My new co-workers were a healthy-looking bunch. They hustled about their duties with a will, and they seemed to be enjoying an easy relationship, laughing and joshing one another. An unbelievable situation in which to find myself. I must have looked particularly pale and emaciated to these men when I started my duties as instructed, sorting packages, looking up names. My fellow workers readily accepted me, asking me about my background and how I happened still to be counted among the living after a year as one of the *Häftlinge* in this place. There were no other Jews in the *Kommando*, but the workers chuckled over my survival account, and I showed them my scars. They began slipping me a variety of foods to sample as we worked. What joy! What delicious and astounding flavors! What was this place, I wondered. Lunch-time was even better. We were not, in contrast to the rest of the camp, on a ration of coarse bread and thin soup. We were served a delicious soup, concocted from many ingredients and cooked on a gas ring in the office. We dined on salamis, cheeses, homemade breads, cakes. I was not long in realizing that an assignment to the *Paketstelle* was an assignment to distribute the contents of an endless cornucopia.

Our *Kommando* was in charge of the packages that arrived daily from anxious loved ones who had been notified that a relative or friend was interned at Auschwitz, Red Cross organizations and governments sent food parcels. Needless to say, many of the addressees were dead, as death was the essential business of this camp. We kept files of the names of all prisoners, living and dead, in the main and sub-camps of Auschwitz. Packages for the living were duly distributed, and at that point the recipient learned his own game of sharing his windfall to gain favors, of knuckling under to pressure from more prominent prisoners. The packages for the dead—those endless packages for the endless dead—were ours to dispose of, a circumstance that put everyone assigned to the *Kommando* in a position of power and wealth. There was the usual hierarchy within, as with all *Kommandos*, and I was on the bottom rung. It was my duty to shine the boots of our SS guard every morning, and to be at the beck and call of my fellow workers at all times. But considering the quality and abundance of food I was now eating, I was satisfied with my flunky status.

Every day we worked at sorting the contents of the packages of the dead: cakes went in one bin, salamis in another, margarine over there, schmaltz (chicken fat, and usually from the Poles) and other perishables in jars were placed here. Cookies had yet another compartment. Many of the vegetables were taken once a day to the kitchen, some to be thrown into the daily soups for the camp. The more delectable items were always kept aside for the use of the post office workers, who, in turn, supplied the Nazi camp administrators as desired.

My co-workers, I observed, walked frequently back and forth from the post office to their barracks. It soon dawned on me that they were helping themselves to a cut of the spoils, and they did so openly, as if this practice were not only accepted but expected. At first, I requested permission to take food for my own use. The *Kapo* allowed me to choose only certain plentiful items. Camp rations were never served at the post office. We did our own cooking within our own quarters, and shared the results with our SS guard. He, too, was content as he did not have to lift a finger to have any food or service he desired. He sat in a nearby office all day long, reading newspapers, listening to the radio, talking with other guards. A constant stream of visitors poured through our office: guards, prominent prisoners, administrators. It occurred to me only gradually why we had so many visitors.

As I polished his boots each morning, our guard even engaged me in small talk, an exchange unheard of in other parts of the camp. During one of our morning sessions, he broached the subject of politics and started to tell me how a fellow named Anton A. Mussert, a Dutch fascist leader, was a great man who was doing many good things for the Dutch people. I was foolish enough to tell him that I did not want to hear about it, that there was no way we could have a fair discussion of the subject since I was his political prisoner, a Dutch Jew, and compelled to shine his boots. He ended his discourse there and then in polite silence, acknowledging, perhaps, that I had a point. I walked away marveling that the guard did not kick my face in as would have happened in similar situations elsewhere in the camp. The guard had taken my reprimand with grace.

How did I stumble into the Paketstelle? During the months I served in the camps and for quite a few years thereafter, I spent no time at all pondering my experiences. I had lived through them, sometimes by luck, and sometimes by trying very hard to live. I was proud that I had lived, and still am. I may have been the only Jew ever admitted to the *Kommando*. The others were mostly criminals and politicals of many years' experience in the camp. In the fall of 1944, however, when I emerged from my long hospitalization and was assigned by the whim of the *Atbeitskapo* to the *Paketstelle*, the atmosphere of the camp was changing. There was an unspoken comprehension that the war was drawing to a close, and that the Third Reich was being defeated. The gas chambers, which had worked at a frantic pace through many months of 1944, were slowing down as the Nazis ran out of large populations of captured Jews for their annihilation plants. Fervent anti-Semitism within the camp began to lessen. I, a Jew, was now being admitted to the ranks of the privileged; that is, if I were discreet, maintained a sense of humor, and made myself useful. I no longer had to scurry with sharpened wits for an extra finger or two of soup or an extra chunk of bread. I ate well. I was in a position to reward others with gifts of food or to barter some of it for things I wanted.

License to steal food was a marvellous experience for a long-starved prisoner. I helped keep the SS guards supplied by relaying their requests to the *Kapo* in charge: a pound of butter, a salami, a cake of a certain type. These things were set aside within the office and, when the guard went off duty, he took the food out of our office concealed in his clothes. In those days, he was probably

The Paketstelle Kommando, 1944

receiving better food through Auschwitz's supply line than he could obtain at home. The situation was farcical. The average prisoner was always scrambling for extra food. If he worked outside the gates and managed to beg some food from a civilian he worked beside, that food was often taken away from him during a body search at the gate. Prisoners could receive food packages from the *Paketstelle* only if they were specifically addressed to them. The rules of the camp were carefully maintained. Administrative personnel were forbidden to help themselves to this food, but the prisoners making up our privileged *Kommando* were not in a position to refuse Nazi requests to help them smuggle food out.

After several weeks at this work, I was assigned to the barracks of the elite like all prominent prisoners who served the elite. Because I served the elite I was now prominent and, in my new barracks, was given a private *Stube*, a tiny cubicle, to myself. It was equipped with a single bunk with warm blankets, even bed sheets, and there was a tiny kitchen closet which contained a hot plate and storage space for my stolen food. I had soap and towels. Washing facilities were easily available, and I was clean again, no longer worried about lice.

That I was now admitted to the barracks of the elite did not fill me with pangs of guilt, not after what I had seen and lived through. The separation of prominent prisoners from the rest of the camp was undoubtedly necessary to keep the administration machinery from being sabotaged. Therefore, anyone who worked among the elite was destined to share their privileges. My feelings as a man, a Dutch national, and a Jew were suppressed except for quiet expressions of defiance such as my exchange with the SS guard about the Dutch fascist, Mussert. I felt good that I was winning the battle of survival; weightier thoughts I did not ask of myself.

After my first shock of amazement, I accepted the new turn of events in my life just as I had accepted the survival tightrope I walked each day as a prisoner. So far I had succeeded at keeping my balance. The fortunes of my prison existence could just as easily have turned the other way at the whim of anyone in authority over me. The choice before us prisoners was always to accommodate to what was ordered or to die. For over a year I had been coerced by means of starvation and ill-treatment. Now I was being coerced with delicious foods and personal privileges.

Our food bought us tailored prison uniforms. The Auschwitz grey and blue stripes were transformed by inmate tailors into well-fitting suits with hand-printed prison numbers on the left pocket of the jacket and the right side of the trouser leg. The belt fitted snugly. Socks and handkerchiefs were *organisiert* for us. We wore leather shoes. The stripes of our uniforms were aligned to match perfectly at the seams. The caps were constructed just as carefully. We thought ourselves walking fashion plates; and, because of the elegant craftsmanship of my clothing, I sometimes almost managed to forget I was still in prison uniform and still a prisoner.

Mornings, the inmates of my new barracks did not fall out at an early hour with the rest of the camp for inspections and countdowns. We rose for work after the other *Kommandos* had marched out of the camp. Our *Blockälteste* would check us off personally every day without ever lining us up to be counted. At the post office we hung our jackets on a nail to begin work before our guard arrived. Daily he lined us up for a formal count, but absences were passed over when the *Kapo* supplied an excuse. We were around the camp somewhere, everyone knew, and so the *Paketstelle* was run more by "gentlemen's agreement" than camp orders.

Walking across the camp any day, I would be stopped by some SS guard who would call me by name. Taking off my cap and coming to attention I would hear him say, "Hey, Max, how about a salami!" or a similar request. I would promise him what he wanted within a certain period of time, then see that he got it. Just as I did errands in my own self-interest for the SS, so fellow prisoners did errands for me for handouts of food. In my new barracks, however, I was now out of contact with most prisoners, and discouraged from contacts outside my *Kommando*.

The Paketstelle Kommando, 1944

My body filled out rapidly. I felt well, fit, and strong. The scars of my pneumonia and abcessed appendicitis were healed and behind me. I was now well dressed by day, warm at night. I even had cigarettes. Since there was no bed-time curfew for our barracks, my co-workers and I often played chess or other games for hours. But my mind was restless as it tried and failed to sort some desperate thoughts. I made a point of getting along, but kept those thoughts to myself, sharing no confidences.

A whorehouse—served, I suppose, by prison women—existed on the second floor of an administration building that stood just inside the entrance gate. The SS guards had free access to the house, and prominent criminal prisoners, *Blockälteste,* and *Kapos* could earn chits as behavior awards toward use of the whorehouse once a month. The whorehouse was not available to Jews, but we glimpsed the women occasionally as one or another appeared at a window or as they were marched some place under guard, as to the medical building.

At Christmas time of 1944, the *Paketstelle Kommando* met together to decide what to give the SS commander of Auschwitz as a Christmas gift. The *Kapo,* an elite prisoner, suggested that a silver tea service would make a fine gift, and, needless to say, we all agreed. Probably, the tea service was ordered by the *Kapo* and our SS guard who had access to a grapevine leading outside the camp. Each of us was asked to put aside some of the best food delicacies that we processed daily in order to pay for our proposed gift.

Piece by piece the silver service began to arrive in our office, and with each addition word was passed around our *Kommando* to bring forth so much in the foods each of us had set aside for the purpose of payment. To my knowledge, except for our guard, the other SS men who visited us regularly for food handouts were unaware of this transaction.

After the entire service had arrived, we polished the pieces in secret, then packed them in a large crate. Carefully bathed and in clean uniforms, we pushed off with a flatbed cart bearing our crate. Our SS guard shepherded our group out through the main gate and toward the nearby home of the camp commander. There the commander of Auschwitz camp invited the *Kapo* and the SS guard into his house, where, reportedly, he very graciously accepted our *Kommando's* gift of a silver tea service paid for in the stolen food of camp victims.

A LAST TRANSPORT FROM AUSCHWITZ JANUARY 1945

On New Year's Eve, December 31, 1944, the *Paketstelle* workers threw one last celebration before my rose-colored world as a wheeler-dealer in Auschwitz fell apart.

The Third Reich was being routed and the overrunning of Auschwitz was expected; no one knew this better than our *Kommando*, who received first-hand information from prominent prisoners working in the SS administration. Word came down that prisoners would be evacuated shortly to other work camps.

By now the prison was beginning to empty. The gas chambers had been efficient, and there were few people left who were not able-bodied workers. During 1944, there had been seemingly endless large transports arriving filled with Hungarian and Italian Jews. These people were in very bad physical condition, as if they had been starved and maltreated for a long period somewhere else. The SS lost no time in causing most of them to disappear. After that, fewer and fewer transports arrived, and gassings fell off sharply. We assumed that the Nazis were running out of victims.

At the time of the Russian offensive on the Eastern

front in 1944, all criminal and political prisoners, but not the Jews, had been called out and offered an opportunity to enlist in the Waffen SS on the condition that they would serve at the Russian front. All criminal records of those who would enlist were promised to be expunged. A number of prisoners accepted, especially the green insignias (criminals). Many spit on the offer, particularly the red insignias (politicals).

What we *Paket* workers did not know was that the SS were beginning to look at all of us able-bodied men with new eyes. We were usable labor for their war plants and industries, seasoned replacements for their own thinning manpower. The maintenance of a death camp on the scale of Auschwitz was no longer necessary or even desirable.

The *Paket* workers celebrated the coming of 1945 like everyone else facing the blank canvas of a new year. We anticipated our liberation but there were events to come that we could not anticipate. We ordered from the prison kitchen a huge vat of ersatz coffee. The prisoners who staggered over with it and up the stairs to the room where the party was held were paid liberally in food. In like manner, we obtained a tankard of schnapps from the town, paying our providers in valuable food. Schnapps was dubious stuff, we all knew, for there was no way of knowing what kind of alcohol and other flavorings had been dumped into it. But who cared? The workers were hankering for a good drunk.

The coffee and schnapps were mixed together, then passed around by the cupfull. Our choicest edibles, which we had all saved for this occasion, were also passed around and eaten in great quantities. I could hardly swallow a mouthful of the beverage that had been concocted, never having developed a taste for coffee, much less alcohol. Nevertheless, I made what I thought was a good show of it, and stuck to eating as my personal means of overindulgence.

The schnapps did have the effect of loosening tongues and inhibitions, including mine. If all the *Kommando* workers were going to open up and say what they wanted, so was I, and I looked forward to the free-for-all.

Conversation zeroed in on the question foremost in our minds: What would be our fate here in Auschwitz as Germany fell to defeat? Each man had his own theory.

One man pointed out that we all knew that the Russians were damn close and that all prisoners had been ordered evacuated. But, he wondered, would our *Kommando* leave too?

Another did not think so because we were prominent members of the camp and were needed to help run the camp. He thought we would be kept as long as possible along with the *Blockälteste, Kapos,* and doctors.

Another: Well, but what happens when the Russians are at the gate? What will the SS do?

Another: We should start thinking about defending ourselves. They may decide to kill us.

Another: I don't think it's going to come to that. The SS will abandon the prison and leave us as a welcoming committee for the Russians. We'll be all right. We're prisoners, aren't we?

So went the nervous conjecture. Events, however, continued to run their course in spite of any independent thoughts we might have. Transports of prisoners were marched out of the camp until, just as some of us had figured, we were among a few *Kommandos* left.

By the middle of January, the camp was almost deserted.. Our daily routines fell apart. We continued our work in a half-hearted manner, but devoted much of our time to helping ourselves to the food we processed, stockpiling it against an uncertain future. There were very few prisoners left, but food packages addressed to great numbers of the dead or evacuated poured into the camp from agencies and governments. We still did not know what the SS had in store for us, and tension mounted day by day. Excitement swelled as we began to hear the sounds of distant artillery fire, then heard it grow louder with each passing day. Evenings brought more drinking bouts, more speculation, but less reliable news as our information grapevine withered.

On a Sunday morning in mid-January, all those still in the camp, except the hospitalized, the doctors, and orderlies, were ordered abruptly out onto the main square. There were several hundred of us. We were told to get our belongings together immediately and to be ready to march out by 1 PM. We scrambled for our barracks to gather our clothing and food. We had each put by so much food and so many articles of clothing and housekeeping that we had purchased with our wealth of food that we were now faced with quick and painful decisions about what to bring and what to abandon. Then we chose partners for the manning of flatbed carts. After putting siding around the flatbeds, we stacked them high with our food. We had *organisiert* rucksacks and other carrying gear for our personal belongings. These we filled and strapped to our backs. As we were called into rough formation and told to start marching, we must have been a ludicrous sight. In tailor-made prison garb, wearing haircuts of one center stripe, we strong prisoners sweated with the effort of pushing and guiding our food-laden carts out onto unfenced roads. Armed SS guards in their green uniforms accompanied us, taking the shoulders of the road as we took the middle. Some of the prisoners pushed the guards' carts, which were lighter by far than those of our *Kommando*.

At first we made nervous jokes, facing the unknown. So far, they had not shot us, but where in hell were we going? For hours we staggered along a deserted road through brown and snow-flecked fields. The loaded carts were all but breaking our backs. We ate endlessly as we marched, but seemed hardly to put a dent in our supplies. The guards had noticeably poorer and fewer rations than we. Soon we began to throw cans in their direction. We knew they had their hands full carrying their guns and would have difficulty opening cans as they marched, then eating from the cans with forks. I giggled over their predicament. The guards seemed to have become the prisoners of the prisoners as we left Auschwitz, dependent as they were on us for food.

Our relationship to our guards as we left Auschwitz was, indeed, a strange one. Since the prison system had called for utilizing prisoners for all labor, the *Paketstelle Kommando* controlled incoming food gifts until the day we left camp. The guards who marched out with us carried only the meager rations issued to them. Access to our better food depended on the good will of the *Paket* workers. Our SS guards walked on either side of us with their guns, but they made no effort to shoot or overpower us for our supplies. For them the writing was on the wall. The Russians were not far behind. Our guards hastened us along. They seemed intent on delivering us to an ordered destination while there was still time. If the Russians caught up with us, the guards could do worse than surrender some well-fed prisoners pulling carts of food. However it came out for the guards, we prisoners hoped the Russians would overtake us.

I cannot remember whether we marched for one or two days or where, if at all, we slept. In time our strength began to give out, and our food-laden carts seemed to grow heavier with every hour we pushed them, even as we continued eating from them. The longer we struggled with our carts the less our precious cargo meant to us. We pitched cans into the ditches, first, one by one, then in fusillades. The guards scampered to retrieve what they could. The rest lay where they were thrown, chance bonuses for passersby.

Our march ended at a railroad siding. There we slumped to catch our breath while watching freight cars being switched into position on the tracks before us. We were given permission to bring with us everything we could carry as we entered the cars. Burdened with packets of food and clothing, we shoved along among a crowd of prisoners into various freight cars, all of which were open to the sky. In the herding process most comrades were separated. I was pushed into a car among strangers. We sat jammed together, barely able to move. I was warmly dressed but the January weather was bitter cold. The closeness of the bodies around me was not unwelcome.

The train moved off to begin its slow roll across the bleak Silesian countryside. The rail joints underneath us clicked a lazy rhythm. I stood up to look around, and spotted the guards in a car ahead of us, the car with machine guns resting their muzzles at the top of the siding. We ate. We talked a little, mostly speculating as usual about where we were headed. Day turned to night as we rolled. Dawn broke on haggard, unsleeping prisoners. Snow fell, swirling around us overhead, settling thickly only when we stopped. And the train squealed to a halt often, sometimes for hours. Conversation ceased altogether in time. The cold was so intense that each of us had to concentrate all of his energy on trying to stay warm. Time and again our prison train was pulled into a siding so that a troop or supply train could get through. We were cleared for another stretch of track only when no other train was expected.

Snow continued to fall on our exposed bodies. Our clothing was wet, frozen in places, and stinking. There was not so much as a can to use as a toilet, and we sat in our own and one another's filth. Each of us had his own rations, but many men began to lose interest in eating. I concentrated hard on staying awake, and forced myself to eat from time to time. Each of us was alone in his misery, the effort at communication long since given up.

Several days passed before we rolled to a stop at a station. Boots pounding a wooden platform and loud shouts were heard. The doors to our car were unbolted and flung open, and we were ordered out. Painfully and stiffly I pulled myself erect. Looking about, I began to see with my eyes what I had only dimly suspected in the numb last days on the train: most of my traveling companions were not asleep. They were dead. I was one of only a few in our car who had not frozen to death. I looked around me at all of the dead, and felt almost nothing. That I was alive in the midst of these dead was the important thing. Death was easy. If I had closed my eyes and given my weary body over to rest as these frozen men had, I, too, would have been dead. If I had not had the luck to be assigned to the *Paketstelle* in the months just passed, I, too, would have lacked the strength to stay awake and alert and alive. As ordered, I stood on my feet, then began to move my reluctant joints and work at restoring my circulation.

This was Max Garcia in early 1945, at the age of 20. It is hard for me to think now, decades later, of how to explain to my children that I had become almost immune to pity for the dead. I had lived the prior year and a half in an atomsphere where death was an accepted resident. The only thing of importance was life because death was more common than life. Life was shown to have little value. Only your own determination could give it value. If you gave in to your mental or physical suffering, if you lost interest, you would die. More than anything you had to want to live, and this became a fearful drive, causing you to seek life on almost any terms. Yet, I think, in the total scheme of things, maybe this is the way nature wants it. You do not know your destiny, and in circumstances like ours in 1944-45, you did not give much for destiny. The important thing was that you woke up in the morning. That was another day.

MAUTHAUSEN, MELK, AND MARCH TO EBENSEE FEBRUARY, MARCH 1945

Those of us Auschwitz prisoners who could move were prodded from the cars by rough new guards and hastened along with heavy blows of their truncheons. Our baggage was immediately confiscated. I could see that I was about to experience all over again my reception as a new prisoner at Buna almost two years before, except that this time I thought I knew what to expect.

Our new prison was at Mauthausen, a small Austrian

Mauthausen, Melk, and Ebensee 121

town near Linz, just above the Danube River and 155 kilometers west of Vienna. Our new guards, the elite prisoners of the camp, set upon us with ferocity, beating us mercilessly. We, the prominent and elite prisoners of Auschwitz, were easily singled out for special punishment, we who had well-fleshed bodies, tailor-made uniforms, good shoes, and numerous possessions. Most of us were reduced in a hurry to prisoners without status. There were a few exceptions: Auschwitz elites who had been criminal or political prisoners in various camps for many years and had friends among the elites of Mauthausen. For the most part these were the men who had been exempt in Auschwitz from having to wear the prison stripe haircut and who could affect the style of the SS guards.

Predictably, we started our routine here by being herded through the camp to the delousing baths. Our clothes were taken from us and we were shoved through the familiar processes of cold showers and the scrubbing of our hairy parts with lysol-filled brushes. Lined up naked on the grounds of the camp in the cold, early-February air, we awaited the recording of our tattooed numbers and the issuance of clothing. Some old rags were eventually flung our way, just as at Buna; and, huddling and shivering together, we crept into whatever we were given.

The Mauthausen I saw in early 1945 appeared to be a holding and dispersal center for prisoners. Prisoners jammed the camp and filled the barracks to overflowing. The rations of the *Häftlinge* seemed more scanty than ever. My gut once again started a useless rebellion against unrelieved hunger. Nausea, pain, and dizziness gripped me, and I became listless. For me, hope had turned to despair, apprehension to mortal fear. Like every other prisoner, I responded mechanically to orders. Blows rained on our backs, heads, and legs as we were herded out of our barracks for daily countdowns, or into soup lines. I was very tired. I noticed little about the routines of the camp or how it was set up.

Thus we waited glumly while our numbers were checked out against whatever records came through to prison authorities at Mauthausen. Within a week's time, we former Auschwitz prisoners were officially reidentified, then reassigned to work camps where our labor was needed. I spent probably less than two weeks at Mauthausen, one of many prisoners in an overcrowded barracks building, beaten and abused routinely, but given no camp duties. One day my number was sounded in a list of numbers being called out for immediate transport. I soon found myself among a truckload of prisoners being driven to a camp not far distant, at the edge of the town of Melk, also on the Danube and due east of Mauthausen. As I left Mauthausen I no longer anticipated my liberation. I was struggling to believe that I could live that long. I barely looked up at the buildings and grounds of the camp at Melk as our trucks lumbered to a stop inside the gates. We prisoners filed down from the trucks and steeled ourselves for the usual blows that accompanied orders to us. No blows came. At Melk, we were ordered to work almost immediately, but we were not beaten or otherwise abused.

After Mauthausen, Melk was a pleasant camp, small and orderly. We were assigned to daily work shifts, the routines of which I no longer recall. What stands out in my memory was the absence of brutality there. We ate the typical meager rations of a cup of tea, a bowl of soup, and a hunk of bread each day, so I was still hungry and dreamed often of the foods I had been compelled to leave behind me at the train. But the camp atmosphere seemed almost friendly, the pace restful. Gradually, we prisoners regained some strength. I began to live once more for the day of my liberation.

Abruptly then, we were moved again. Our internment at Melk had lasted no longer than a month. The Russians were advancing once more. It must have been March when all of this camp were evacuated. Open motorized barges carried thousands of prisoners up the Danube. I was among them, retracing our journey of a month before, but this time in the opposite direction, by water, and passing Mauthausen. We landed at the town of Linz.

Filing from the barges at a bridge, we were told by SS

guards that we were to start a march of a few days to the next camp. At the same time we were handed rations for the trip which were surprisingly generous in amount: two loaves of bread, some margarine, and a salami. This was an unheard-of bonus, even for a long march, and many of us saw in it another good sign that the end was at hand, that there was the possibility of our being overtaken by the Russians at any moment. I was excited. This was my third move within two months. I started our march confidently, but just in case liberation was still further off than I was hoping, I kept a firm grip on my loaves and my salami. The terrain was not difficult, and I was in good shape. Within twenty-four hours, however, the strength of many prisoners was flagging, and our walking slowed to a shuffle. We slept, or tried to, along the roadsides, stopping at the edges of streams or at farmhouses for water. Altogether we walked for three days and two nights.

General weakness and exposure took their toll, but mentally most of us were alert. We believed we had the stamina to outlast our captors. I was a survivor among an army of survivors. Few of us had developed close friendships, but we all gave a hand to stragglers—those older or weaker ones who were having difficulty keeping up. When we moved too slowly, the SS guards prodded us to move faster. The road climbed into higher country near Gmunden, then wound alongside a long lake. We pulled our weaker comrades along, not wanting to give the SS the satisfaction of watching a single one of us go down. We hiked, at long last, into and through the town of Ebensee, then up a last difficult mountain road to our camp. We were exhausted but inwardly triumphant that every last prisoner had made it to our destination, that not one of them had been shot as a straggler or died of neglect along the way.

Arriving among thousands on the *Appellplatz* of Ebensee, I felt that we had scored a major victory over our enemy, that our successful march was a sign that no more of us would die before our liberation. My euphoria was soon punctured. I looked about me at an already incredibly crowded prison camp. A sea of gaunt and filthy inmates eyed us hopelessly.

One more time we were sent off to the usual shower and delousing routine. We were packed into barracks that were already crowded with prisoners, and assigned to sleep two to a bunk in tiers of bunks, four high. Food rations were thin and of poor quality. We could not rest and starvation dogged us all.

Treated like a menagerie of hated animals, driven mercilessly and beyond our strength to work in a mountainside factory, we lived, each of us, on hope of imminent liberation. Many were the prisoners who gave up that hope, and then their bodies. Daily the *Totenkommando* came around to carry the dead off to the crematorium. I got through the nightmarish days and nights of Ebensee Camp one by one. It was fortunate that I did not know that the liberation of our camp was five or six weeks away.

PART 4

SERVING AMERICAN FORCES IN EUROPE

Max R. Garcia as a member of the Nurnberg C.I.C. unit, 1946.

THE 319TH INFANTRY REGIMENT 1945—1946

The officers and men of the First Battalion, 319th Infantry Regiment, did not expect my return from Holland, but when I was back among them they accepted me as if I were back from military leave. Gratefully, I resumed duty in Intelligence and Reconnaisance. My former bed awaited me in the pretty German house that had become our platoon quarters.

The quiet routines of the 319th continued as if I had not left. We rotated duty, cleaned quarters on schedule, attended drills and orientation movies, walked the downtown streets, and played baseball and catch for exercise. Evenings we spent in a makeshift enlisted men's club, or at American movies, or scheming to meet local girls. On Sundays our regimental band played for both GI's and townspeople in the Bad Wörishofen park bandshell. Groups of GI musicians spelled each other, playing the latest American big-band tunes in various styles, drawing crowds of summer strollers as their admiring audience. After the USO moved in, the musicians played jazz and big-band combos in a clublike setting. Occasional entertainers from the States brought out the whole outfit as an audience; our day-to-day entertainment staples, however, were the old recorded favorites and new record releases provided by the USO. But of all the benefits of the USO, the most popular was that GI's could meet girls there. The meetings took place under chaperoned conditions, but what went on when the club closed for the night was up to the couples.

"Fraternization," as intimacy with the girls of occupied enemy territories was called, although forbidden by Army policy, was the only real game in town. Everyone had a German girlfriend who wanted candy bars, cigarettes, small luxury items, and the company of young men in army uniform—everyone, that is, except me. I was called upon right and left to translate between American men and German women, or to speak to a particular German girl in behalf of some GI. I met many a woman looking for companionship, and yet I could not bring myself to want intimacy with any German woman. I responded stiffly to their overtures and turned away from them in disgust. The women kept smiling and my friends either laughed at me or worked on me with persuasive arguments. "Hell, Max, the Germans were America's bitter enemy too, not just yours, and we're damned glad we finally brought them to their knees. But why bring the women into it? Women are the same everywhere. They're not fighters. They want to be given things and treated right, and then they'll do right by you." After a few weeks of trying to counter arguments of this nature when I had not begun to figure out what women were all about, I lost my fastidiousness and my virgin state all at the same time. Sexual encounters were everywhere for the asking, and I joined the merry-go-round of fraternization with available German girls.

Possibly to give the occupying army something else to think about, and to reinstill habits of military discipline, the commanding general ordered a divisional field parade. Our regiment had paraded down the main street of Bad Worishofen like any other military unit. The GI's had marched with shouldered rifles, flags flying, bands playing. The townspeople had turned out at curbside to watch. But the field parade was an American phenomenon I had not heard of. Conceived as an instructive exercise drill for units in the area, some thousands strong, the parade was an enormous undertaking. Once the date was set, officers buried themselves in the detailed logistics of planning the convocation of all units and their equipment, of scheduling their exercises, their individual rendezvous stations, their feeding.

Because the parade was held on our home territory, the men of the 319th were delegated to find a suitable site. We found flat pasture land that fully met our requirements. Accompanying a delegation as interpreter, I told the farmer-owner that his land was being requisitioned for a brief period, that he could graze his cattle there only when American troops were not using it. We ripped up his fences so that tanks, armored trucks, and artillery vehicles could enter. We staked out the field, marking the spots where various units would line up. Spectators to the field parade were welcome but no one ordered the local population to attend. Even so, on the scheduled day, Germans left their nearby towns to gather in crowds at the site. Each unit of the 80th Division, with its armored equipment, was ordered by the Commanding Officer to pass in review. One by one, the units marched and rolled past the reviewing stand in a continuous flow, an impressive spectacle of energy and power. All units had come together in the early morning hours from their scattered bases in the surrounding countryside. After passing the reviewing stand, they left the area in a predesignated order to return to their home territories. The Germans, too, filed quietly back to their homes.

Routine settled in again. I looked for chores to keep me busy. Idleness was not for me; it allowed my mind to wonder about tomorrow and to grow anxious. Max Garcia, needed aide to the 319th, was how I preferred to see myself. I had no other identity and wanted no other. I had spent my young manhood working to survive. It suited me now to work at serving in any way I could these open-hearted, strong Americans who had given me food, shelter, and open companionship. If anything was wanted or needed in the regiment, I would find a way to get it. I was kidded about my survival tactics and my old-world ways. I would shoot back wisecracks about the foibles of American GI's, but I was genuinely glad to be called upon to translate, or to explain some local matter, or to apply my knowledge of *Organisierung* to obtain a hard-to-get article. Called "the Dutchman," I was fairly well known in the outfit.

Back in Aich Assach I had acquired my first camera. I began to take snapshots of the men of my company, a hobby I continued in Bad Wörishofen. I snapped pictures of them at march and drill. I snapped my friends at rest, in quite different moods. There were Marksberry, McDonald, Pritchett of I. & R.; GI friends Beer, Kullowitz, McCarthy; officers Miles, Salomone, Regan, Poppen, Schmalz, and McWhorter. Some of us toured nearby towns in our off-duty hours. My curiosity and my camera then turned to interesting local buildings, notable details and wall paintings, sculptures, parks, and fountains. I looked inquisitively at structures quite different in character from the close, narrow buildings of Dutch and Belgian cities.

One day I was called to headquarters. Some of the officers drove me out to their new club, which was being established in an old country inn. They showed me their remodeling work, then called my attention to the bar that was being constructed. The club was to open the forthcoming Saturday night, they told me, and when it did they wanted the bar to be equipped in a typically American way, meaning, they explained, that not only drinks were to be served there but bowls of hard-boiled and pickled eggs. No one had seen a fresh egg since our arrival in Bad Wörishofen. The men had grumbled continually about the reconstituted powdered eggs served daily for breakfast. Now the officers longed for at least a few fresh eggs for the opening night of their American-style bar.

"Max, it would sure be great if you could find us some fresh eggs," one of them suggested. "There just have to be a few chickens hidden around here somewhere."

"Yes, sir. If it's eggs you want, I'll bet I can find some," I said. One of the cooks was assigned to drive with me in a jeep. We drove around and through a number of small farms. To our inquiries, farmers shook their heads about where laying chickens might be found. We drove back to town, discouraged, but vowing to take our search farther the next day. Driving down one street of the town, however, I spotted a building which aroused my curiosity when I noticed that a number of women were entering and leaving it regularly. We stopped to watch. The women entering were carrying folded-up bags. Those leaving carried bags filled with something, something delicate, for they carried the bags carefully. Eggs, I thought. They carry them just as our customers used to when they bought eggs at our poultry store in Amsterdam.

"Wait here," I told my companion. "I think we've got something." I jumped out of the jeep and walked into the building. Many women were lining up inside, and what they were there to buy became immediately obvious. The place was an egg warehouse. Eggs were racked from floor to ceiling. I could hardly believe what my eyes were seeing. I ran out to tell the cook about my find.

"You know why we're eating powdered eggs?" I asked. "Because the God-damned Germans have stockpiled every egg in Germany, that's why. That place is full of eggs."

I asked the cook to get a truck while I went back inside to take over the warehouse. "Max, you're crazy," the cook said. We can't do that. All we need is a few eggs. The officers will never go for stealing a warehouse full of eggs."

"Then don't tell them. Just bring back a truck and some more GI's and we'll load up."

We argued. I convinced the cook to go after a truck. Re-entering the building, I ordered the owner to sell no more eggs and to dismiss his customers. I told him his egg supply was being confiscated for the use of the American Army.

The owner looked at me in amazement, then spluttered, "These eggs are my property. You can't just take them."

"Mister, you seem to have forgotten who won the war," said I, warming to combat. "You stole from me when you occupied Holland. You stole everyone blind in every country you went to. Don't tell me we can't take your eggs. Get those women out of here!"

We shouted at one another. The women joined in, screaming at me furiously. The truck I had ordered seemed a long time in coming, and I felt progressively more nervous waiting for it in this company. I held my ground. Reluctantly the women began to leave. Finally the jeep returned with a truck behind it. There had been more arguments at headquarters, the cook told me, about the ethics of taking a truckload of eggs, about the probable disapproval of Military Government. Unbelievable, I thought. I was asked to go find some eggs; and when I did, the Americans did not know whether they should take them. Nevertheless, we loaded our truck to capacity.

We drove onto the company street where an amazed crowd gathered to watch the unloading of our truckload of eggs. Crazy Garcia had done it up right this time, they said. The officers would have more eggs than drinks at the opening of their club bar, and plenty would be left for the regulars.

Our commanding officer, Lieutenant Colonel Arthur H. Clark, who had allowed me to cast my lot with the 319th in Aich Assach, came out to survey our haul. I could see that he was amused, but at the same time he expressed concern about how he was going to explain such a heist to Military Government.

I could not understand these Americans, and said so. What was all the agony? What had I learned in my life but that the strong always took from the weak, the victor from the vanquished. The Americans themselves had not hesitated to commandeer housing and land, to bribe women to their uses with food, cigarettes, and clothing. Yet now they were getting balky about taking a supply of eggs. No German or Russian occupation forces would have hesitated.

Beyond my understanding was the concoept that the Americans did not see themselves in the permanent role of military conqueror, that they were beginning to try to forge a fair policy of local self-government so that they could go home.

Right or wrong, with guilt or without, everyone ate the eggs that I had provided. After all, everyone agreed, what could be done about the ways of their dedicated Dutchman.

On Sunday morning following the officers' Saturday-night club opening, the cooks provided a festival of fresh eggs for breakfast. Whatever the preference of the GI—scrambled, boiled, sunny-side-up, over-easy, poached —that's how his eggs were cooked, and in any amount ordered. Some ate six at once. There were eggs for

The 319th Infantry, 1945—1946

breakfast, lunch, and dinner for days, cooked ungrudgingly in any style by cooks who were glad to be able to serve a dish so popular with the men.

The next time the officers asked me to procure a supply of something, they gave me money to pay for it from the Soldiers' Fund. What they wanted in the next instance was wine for the whole unit. The officers had heard that wine was available cheaply in the French Zone of occupation at the German-French border. What with my reputation for bringing home the bacon (as the Americans called it) and my ability to speak both French and German, I was the logical choice to "assist" a wine-finding detail to the border.

A young and eager second lieutenant, named Charles McWhorter, had supervisory charge of the expedition. Two enlisted men also accompanied us, one driving our truck, and one the jeep in which the lieutenant and I rode. We drove North, all the way to Wiesbaden. We found no cheap wine in quantity, but we enjoyed looking around, like four tourists, at the fine old towns we passed through. Some buildings in Wiesbaden had been reduced to rubble a few months earlier. Men in military uniforms and vehicles clogged the streets. We had no trouble finding Bachelor Officers Quarters (BOQ) for Lieutenant McWhorter, and a USO club for the rest of us, where we spent the night. In the morning we pooled the information we had gathered the night before while drinking with Frenchmen and Americans. We headed due south to Baden-Baden. There, as advised, we found our wine suppliers. We bargained, bought, and loaded up. Back on the company street the following night, volunteers were eager to help unload our precious cargo.

Not long after that trip, Colonel Clark received orders to go home. I hated to see him go. There was a formal distance between his high rank and my auxiliary status, but he had taken me in at Aich Assach, had kept his promise to me, and had seen that I was treated well even when I made mistakes. A celebration was planned in his honor at the officers' club on the night he was to leave. Along with his driver, I was delegated to accompany him to a train in another town after the party. At the appointed hour of departure, the driver and I entered the club to pick up the colonel. Everyone was celebrating. Everyone was drunk. Colonel Clark, the center of attention, was hardly sober. Gently we pulled him away, reminding him that he had to make his train connection, and we helped him into the back of his waiting staff car.

Sitting next to the colonel during the long car journey to the station, I summoned the courage to tell him that I would always be thankful that he had taken me into the regiment at Aich Assach, and that I was going to miss him. To my astonishment, Colonel Clark turned to me and said that he was going to help me get to the United States. He knew how much I wanted to go there, and he wanted to help. I was deeply moved, and tried to express my profound gratitude. Then I checked myself. I realized that the colonel probably would not remember for long what he had said to me. I poured coffee from a canteen for Colonel Clark to drink, to help sober him up for the train ride. We made the train on time, shook hands all around, and wished one another well.

I tried to imagine what it would be like to be in Colonel Clark's shoes and able to leave devastated Europe because his tour of duty was up. He would return to his family in prosperous America where everyone was free to do as he liked, where everyone was rich and drove his own car.

By late fall the 80th Division was ordered to Czechoslovakia. Our regiment packed up to travel military-convoy style across Bavaria to northern Czechoslovakia where we pitched camp outside the town of Eger (now called Cheb, Czechoslovakia). To my relief, there had been no question about my coming along. I was an accepted, if unofficial, member of the 319th Infantry Regiment. The 80th Division had been sent in to replace another American occupying force in this territory until such time as an agreement could be worked out with Russia to restore Czechoslovakia as a fully independent state. The Russians, in 1945, occupied most of eastern Czechoslovakia. The Americans occupied the western borderlands, the "Sudetenland," which the Third Reich had annexed in 1938, a move that was welcomed by the German-speaking population of the area. While the Czechs looked upon the Sudeten Germans as traitors for having joined forces with the Nazis, the Sudetens looked upon the Americans as their liberators. The Czechs and Sudetens disliked one another, and the Russians considered all of us their enemies. Thus our occupation duty in Czechoslovakia was of a far more nervous character than duty in Austria had been.

Czechoslovakia had not existed as a nation until the end of World War I when it became independent as one of the succession states of the defeated Austrian-Hungarian empire. In World War II, Czechoslovakia was swallowed up by Hitler—the Sudetenland first, the rest later. Soon after World War II, the Allies persuaded Russia to restore Czechoslovakia as a free nation as the terms of the mutual withdrawal of American and Russian occupying forces. When the 80th Division finally pulled out of Sudetenland, the Russians withdrew their armies to the east, leaving Czechoslovakia an independent republic once more. (But after the Allied presence was gone, the Russians lost little time in bringing Czechoslovakia under their political control. The forced suicide or murder in 1948 of Foreign Minister Jan Masaryk signaled the triumph of Moscow-dominated communism in Czechoslovakia. From that time on, she has been counted among the puppet states of the U.S.S.R.)

In late 1945, the 319th assumed a posture of military readiness as they settled down in Sudetenland. The rookies sent into the regiment to replace homeward-bound combat veterans were drilled daily and put through maneuvers alongside the regulars. Neglected rifles were oiled. Makeshift telephone lines were strung between all units of the 80th Division.

In time we became familiar with the customs, problems, and people of our Sudeten locale. I met some of the citizens of Eger soon after our arrival when I was assigned to find a baker to prepare our unit's bread. Talking to townspeople in order to place orders for bread, rolls, cakes, and such, I began to pick up some Czech words. Like everyone else in the unit, I also found words to pick up some Czech girls. Manless since the departure of the Nazis, and deprived of the favors they had received under Nazi occupation, many Sudeten girls were now eager to fraternize with the Americans. Often hated by their fellow citizens, these girls looked to the Americans for sexual companionship and the amenities that followed.

The whole battalion was quickly overrun with girls. The officers were as vulnerable as the men. They had to issue restrictive orders, but they turned away from enforcement. To get around the prohibition of women in enlisted men's quarters, the GI's hired their girlfriends to clean the barracks, paying them in Army scrip. In this way, the women entered a paid domestic arrangement that was condoned by the officers. In fact, the officers cooperated to the extent of giving notice well in advance as to when the inspections would be held in the enlisted men's quarters.

We performed our occupation duties as ordered; but, just as in Bad Worishöfen, we reserved our greatest energy for eating, drinking, dancing, making love, and changing partners. No doubt the Russian occupiers not so far away were playing the same game.

I ate my first American Thanksgiving dinner in Eger with the 319th. It was an orgy of formal dining courses, the like of which I had never seen or tasted. My preoccupation with foods, a habit since my days in the prison camps, was lively. In the months of my attachment to American forces, I had always cultivated a close relationship with the cooks and their kitchens, and enjoyed assignments to obtain local foods from local suppliers. Noticing the arrival of large, extra cartons of foodstuffs starting in early November, I hung around the kitchen to find out why supplies were increasing. The cooks told me about the history and traditions of the American Thanksgiving Day. I watched them cut, cook, and bake for days. Yet I was not prepared for the extravagance of the celebration, even at our distant outpost. On the appointed day, the men were summoned to the mess hall, which had been converted into an elegant dining room. Tables covered with white linen, decorated with candlesticks and centerpieces of fruits, nuts, and flowers, were laid with individual place settings. Serving tables were covered with an unusual array of food. Prayers were offered. Then we dug in. I tasted everything: turkey, stuffing, candied yams, cranberry sauce, peas, carrots, beans, corn, all in sauces or butter, salads, rolls, relishes, pickles, then pumpkin, mince or apple pie.

A month later, we consumed a similar feast in celebration of Christmas. Throughout that season, from Thanksgiving to New Year, American GI's received and shared great boxes of home-cooked baked goods and candies, as well as small gifts.

For the New Year, I jumped into preparations for another wild party, this one under rather different circumstances from the one thrown at Auschwitz the year before. We rented a hotel clubroom for the occasion, and I hired a German brass band. Liquor rations had been saved up. On New Year's Eve, the mess sergeant and I set up serving tables, stocking them with rows of popular American liquor brands, sodas, and cans of fruit juices. There was very little beer because the beer-producing areas, such as Pilsen, were occupied by the Russians.

In my efforts to Americanize, I had tried but had not succeeded in developing their capacity for downing hard liquor. This night was no exception. We had been asked to attend the party in full-dress uniform, and had permission to bring our *Fräuleins*. Because I was planning to help, my girl and I arrived early. We mixed our liquor with various delicious juices. We danced, we socialized, and drank more cocktails. By the time most of my friends arrived, I was sitting down and could not get up. Well before midnight I suffered the humiliation of being half-carried, half-dragged back to my barracks bunk. I awoke hours later to find a furious girlfriend sitting reluctantly by my side. As her ticket to the party, I had been a wipeout.

On off-duty hours, many GI's took tours to local resorts and places of interest. I joined excursions to nearby Franzensbad, then Marienbad, where we relaxed in elegant hotels and restaurants, bought souvenirs in pleasant shops, bathed in their famous spa waters, and drank the "therapeutic" mineral waters. The USO arranged a special tour to the venerable capital city of Prague, which was in the Russian Zone of occupation. My request to join that tour was turned down because of the possibility of my being identified and detained by the Russians as a Displaced Person.

Early in 1946, the 80th Division received long expected orders to pull out of Czechoslovakia. The Russians had agreed to pull out as well. To commemorate the end of our occupation and the restoration of freedom to Czechoslovakia, the 319th joined Russian and Czechoslovakian units in a formal military parade down the main street of Eger.

Once more our battalion packed up to join a stream of 80th Division trucks clogging the highways into Germany. We were headed for the town of Aschaffenburg, near Frankfurt, where the troops were to be deactivated. Our camp-following Sudeten girlfriends traveled with us. Terrified of what would happen to them if they stayed behind in free Czechoslovakia, the girls had climbed into some of the trucks for the long ride into the heart of Germany. Once at Aschaffenburg, the entire division was put under quarantine within a tent camp. The girls waited in vain outside the closed camp. They had no money, no food, and no prospects of fraternizing further with the Americans. Called a "repple depple," or replacement depot, the camp served to process home-going servicemen through medical examinations and treatment, prevention shots, and record checking. Passes outside the camp were not issued. Time dragged. The men played cards, lay on their bunks, smoked, or hung about the USO, awaiting orders for shipment home.

I waited too, but not for shipment to the States. Back in Eger I had been snapped into a state of personal anxiety once more when official orders came through for the division to be sent home. As usual, I had postponed thinking about what I would do next until I was forced to think. I went to see Captain Jesse Miles under whom I had worked since Aich Assach. To my relief, he told me that as a career army man he was not due to return to the States, and that his plans included taking me with him to his next assignment. I told him about Colonel Clark's drunken promise to me, and asked if he thought it were possible that the colonel might help me get to the States. Captain Miles suprised me by affirming that he knew of the colonel's intentions, that they had discussed the matter before the colonel left. Colonel Clark had asked Captain Miles to look after me until arrangements could be worked out.

My head reeled. So this had not been the sentimental talk of a friendly officer in his cups. Even if I never reached the States, the humanity of the colonel's efforts for me was overwhelming. I hardly dared hope that the generous efforts of an American officer would give me a future in the United States.

THE C. I. C. 1946

Captain Jesse Miles took me with him from the Aschaffenburg replacement depot to Scheinfeld in Bavaria, where he had been assigned to duty with the 18th Regiment of the First Infantry Division. We found his new unit headquartered in a hilltop castle overlooking the town.

Miles reported to the commanding officer while I sat in the staff car. Some minutes later he returned to escort me into the ornate office of the colonel in charge. The colonel, a full bird, was a short man, even shorter than I, but he had a scrappy manner and two German shepherd dogs. I kept a wary eye on the colonel and his dogs, but the two officers talked over my situation amiably enough. Miles went so far as to explain that he was acting as my guardian for a colonel who was hoping to help me emigrate to the States. He outlined the work I had been doing for the 319th and asked the colonel if he would try to find some work for me in his own I. & R. unit. Without so much as a lowering of the eyebrows, the forbidding looking colonel agreed, and to my relief I started pulling routine duty once more. But I. & R. had become dull work. On-the-spot translating was almost never needed. The bureaucracy of peace was enlarging daily, with ever more specialized agencies engaged in the governing process. I. & R. men at the regimental level had to scratch hard for something to do.

Bitter winds blew snow about the turrets of our castle and down into her courtyards. We kept our coats on in the castle's vast, cold rooms. Within a few weeks I no longer saw details of the interior that had so impressed me on our arrival: marble staircases and statuary, richly polished woods throughout, massive and ornate furnishings, and, in one large hall, individual ceiling frescoes framed within heavy intersecting beams. Heedless of the opulence, our regiment festooned the castle rooms and halls with communications wiring, and filled the picturesque courtyard with trucks.

Often, on off-duty hours, we drove down to Scheinfeld and through her classic entrance-tower gate in order to stroll about this quaint Bavarian town. Evenings we gathered to drink and socialize at the local enlisted men's club. At one such gathering I met and talked with a GI who became extremely interested when I mentioned my background. He asked me many questions about what I had been through and when we parted I realized that he had learned a great deal more about me than I had about him.

Within a few days he sent me an invitation to a dinner sponsored by the local unit of the Counter Intelligence Corps. Pondering the reasons for such an invitation, I became wary enough to seek out Captain Miles. I asked the captain what he could make of a GI pumping me for my story, then asking me to a dinner for C.I.C. agents. I feared a trap and that my attendance at the dinner would result in my being sent to a D.P. camp or back to Holland. Miles was surprised to hear of the C.I.C. overture, but he looked at the invitation and thought over the fears I had expressed. He said he doubted that the C.I.C. was interested in hunting down D.P.'s who were not war criminals. He suggested that I see their invitation as an interesting opportunity for myself and a possible turning point in my life. He reminded me that I was not doing much at that point besides waiting to hear from Colonel Clark, and I might as well be doing some useful work among interesting people while I waited.

I went to the dinner, joining a small group of young men dressed in officer's pinks, but showing no rank. We talked together as a number of drinks were consumed, followed by an excellent dinner. By dessert I had told my story once more before the assembled group. In answer to my questions they told me a little about the work of the C.I.C., and that they were primarily interested in rounding up Nazis and overseeing the establishment of local civil governments under American Military Government. One person popped the question. Would I consider joining the C.I.C.? My language ability and my I. & R. training were just what they were looking for, he explained, but in addition they had to be assured that I had the motivation to dedicate myself to their kind of work.

I told them that I was not sure, that I would like some time to think about it. Not yet a year out of concentration camps and often barely disguising angry, vengeful impulses toward Germans, I knew I could hunt Nazi war criminals with dedication. On the other hand, the camps had taught me to be wary as a hunted animal myself. I still suspected the C.I.C. might be interested in rounding up D.P.'s still on the loose. Men wandering homeless were a constant problem to occupying forces, and the Americans might be looking to the day when I would be left behind. I did not want to risk being processed back to Holland, particularly with my new hope of emigrating to the United States. I had seen Holland after the war. I, a Jew, would never be at home in Amsterdam again. If I were forced to return what would I do in that war-devastated country to live? I could see the writing on the wall. I would be a diamond polisher, a surviving Jewish diamond polisher, who would teach the trade to a new generation of gentile polishers.

In the end I trusted to Miles' opinion and overcame my fears. I made an appointment with the C.I.C. contact man, telling him that I would take the job provided I was given the same guarantees I had demanded of the 319th. They had to promise not to abandon me if their unit were to move on or to return to the United States. They had to make some provision for my care and safety. The C.I.C. man gave me his solemn word that I would be looked after. He asked me to report for duty the following week.

I began to pack my belongings and to say farewells to the officers and men of the 18th Infantry Regiment. The time was late March. During that week Captain Miles received a letter from Colonel Clark, postmarked Buffalo, New York. Miles ran to my room and showed me the colonel's signed affidavit, dated 7 March 1946, sponsoring my emigration to the United States. I was dumbfounded to realize that Colonel Clark had kept his promise to me, a homeless Jewish refugee. My gratitude and astonishment gave way to pure elation. I turned to Captain Miles and asked him when and how I could plan to leave.

News had reached us by then that President Truman had authorized in December, 1945, the admission to the United States of 42,000 qualifying Displaced Persons. Miles reminded me that to qualify for United States immigration I had to have a visa from my country of origin, and that my case could well be complicated by the fact that I had refused to return to my homeland or to register there or anywhere except with the American Army. In addition, I had just committed myself to new duty with the C.I.C. We talked over my prospects for obtaining a visa, and eventually I agreed with his analysis that if I worked for the C.I.C. for awhile, they could probably help me obtain a visa and passage to the States faster than he could or I could by my own efforts. I agreed to honor my commitment. Captain Miles drove me to the local office of the C.I.C. on the appointed day, and Miles assured me that we could stay in touch.

The C.I.C. 143

At their offices, instead of being invited to unpack, I was hustled with my baggage into a car and driven immediately to Bamberg. I had been given only the briefest of explanations: six weeks of indoctrination and training at Bamberg was standard operating procedure. It sounded logical, but the silent ride to nearby Bamberg was long enough for old anxieties to arise that I might be stepping into a trap.

To my relief, I was greeted warmly and officially at the other end by a couple of officers who called me by name and let me know they were expecting me. They introduced me around, showed me to my room, and gave me a briefing on house rules. Though I had never met a single person at the Bamberg headquarters, each of them made an effort to put me at my ease.

As the C.I.C.'s newest recruit, I joined a curiously assorted group of trainees. Some were American, some European. A few were women. Most of us were in our twenties, but a few were as old as their forties. I could tell where most of my European companions came from by their accents, but we were discouraged from asking personal questions about one another. Only the administrative officers knew our personal histories. Encouraged to keep to ourselves and to avoid fraternizing with even American forces, we settled down to learn and work together. We all dressed now in identical officers' uniforms conspicuously unmarked by rank. We were trained in setting up files, in firing revolvers and the M-45, and in standard military driving procedures. We were instructed in interrogation techniques and various aspects of reconnaissance and counter-intelligence. Much of the material we covered I had learned previously, but never in such scientific detail. I trained no more than four weeks when I was told to pack up for assignment to Nürnberg.

By early May, 1946, a C.I.C. driver delivered me to the door of an imposing city mansion that served as our headquarters in Nürnberg. Again I was warmly received and shown around our vast quarters before being escorted to comfortable rooms across the street. Staff members welcomed me cordially, treating me like an equal in rank and experience. If I was somewhat unsettled not to know who had authority over whom here, I pretended not to be concerned, and within a day or so I no longer cared. I became transformed, as if by magic, into a real officer relaxing at his private club.

I was briefed on the specifics of our work. We were charged with picking up intelligence about actions that might be against the interest of the U.S. Army. We were to ferret out Nazis who ranked in the SS. We were to cooperate closely with Military Government to restore the rudiments of local civil government. Black marketing and local law enforcement, usually outside C.I.C. jurisdiction, were to be followed up if an intelligence angle was suspected.

I started duty by assisting with office interrogations. Nürnberg had its share of Frenchmen, Belgians, and Dutchmen who had supposedly been brought to wartime Germany as forced laborers, but some of whom were Nazi sympathizers who had agreed during the war to work in German factories. Most of these people now wanted to go home. Our task was to determine which ones were Nazis, so that they could be processed through military courts or turned over to their home governments for justice. One of my first assignments was to be called upstairs to assist at the interrogation of a young Dutch couple who claimed to have been brought to Germany as forced labor. For about ten minutes I listened to the interrogator and the couple speak to one another in German. I caught them in a lie about some of their details and stopped the questioning to call for a consultation with the interrogator. We left the room to decide on a strategy, then returned to the questioning of the couple. I suddenly broke into the exchange, speaking in Dutch, and told the two that they were liars and Nazi sympathizers. Taken off guard, the two capitulated and confessed. They begged to be able to return home, stating that they had been too young to know what they were doing, that they learned a bitter lesson by their acts. I wrote a report on the case, after which the Dutch couple were turned over to Dutch government representatives in Nürnberg.

The C.I.C.

We had civilian clothing for undercover work, and a number of us also shared the use of a beautiful Mercedes Benz convertible that the Americans had "liberated" (their term for *Organisiert*). We agents were an almost comical give-away as we rode around town in that convertible, civilian clothes notwithstanding. Everyone knew that the Mercedes belonged to the C.I.C., and that the Americans were almost the only ones in town with enough gasoline to drive such a car.

I drove the Mercedes at every opportunity, feeling like a king as I slid into the smooth leather seat beneath the steering wheel. Looking out over the great headlamps, I would roar off through the streets of Nürnberg, dodging pedestrians, bicycles, and horse carts. I did not need so much as a driver's license to get anywhere I wanted to go in that car.

One day a tip came into the office that a wanted SS officer was due to arrive at the railroad station on a certain train. He was expected to be in civilian clothing, but we had a good photograph of him. A contingent of us agents in civilian clothes packed our revolvers and sped to the station in our well-known Mercedes. We elbowed our way through crowds of homeward-bound P.O.W.'s, and met the train on which our fugitive was supposed to arrive. We thought we spotted him and shouted to him to stop. The man turned swiftly into the crowd, and we shot over their heads in his direction. Everyone dived to the floor, but search as we did, we could not find our man again. Still, we climbed back into the Mercedes in good humor. The chase had been great fun. Even if our quarry had eluded us, we knew we had given him a good scare and that he would have to keep on running.

On another occasion I was sent by myself in one of our jeeps to pick up a former SS officer who had just been identified. The address I was given was that of a butcher store. The store was open but no one was in the front room. No one entered or left the store. I began to sweat as I thought about the man I was after, an SS butcher, who would be working in his back room with a cleaver. For some minutes I peered through the window before I summoned the courage to kick open the door and rush to the back room, revolver in hand. There I found the man I was after, sitting quietly at his kitchen table. I flashed my credentials and announced his arrest. He surrendered without a word, and made no effort to overpower me as I drove with him beside me to headquarters.

I was on night duty when I took a phone call that multiple murders had been committed at a nearby Polish D.P. camp. The C.I.C. was expected to investigate to determine if subersive activities were involved in the crime. At about 10 PM I drove across town to the camp, where I showed my credentials to the Military Police. They escorted me to a cordoned off barracks building, and led me inside to a sickening scene of splattered blood and brains. My stomach churned. I tried hard not to gag as I pulled out my notebook to begin writing up what I saw and interviewing witnesses.

I learned that the D.P.'s at the camp, while awaiting repatriation, were employed as guards at military installations, receiving in exchange occupation chits and cigarettes. To increase their earnings, many of them worked the black market on the side. The D.P.'s wore blue-dyed American uniforms and were housed together in old German military barracks such as the blood-spattered one in which I stood that night. The place was divided into two-bunk cubicles, each with enough extra room for a single chair. Clothes were hung on nails in the partition walls, which were about 1½" in thickness.

According to witnesses, two of the three dead men I had found there had been feuding for weeks over their operations in the cigarette black market. One of them worked himself into such a frenzy of anger that he had obtained a gun. That evening he had aimed it through the wall of his cubicle toward the head of his enemy whom he knew was sleeping on the other side. His bullet killed not only his enemy but the fellow sleeping in the next bunk. When he realized what he had done, the anguished man turned his gun around and blew his own brains out.

Back at headquarters I reported my findings to the duty officer. I had found no evidence of subversive activity, only of frustration, passion, and remorse. I added that I was still sick to my stomach over what I had seen. The duty officer laughed and told me to forget it. He advised me to get over it by eating a bowl of good spaghetti. At breakfast in the morning, agents who had heard about my report greeted me with taunts and laughter over my squeamishness.

Sent out solo again to look into a report of wholesale thefts at a Quartermaster Corps supply depot, which was also guarded by D.P.'s, I drove to the area of inquiry and poked about in order to observe the action. I was spotted by the commanding officer, a colonel, who summoned me to his office and asked me to identify myself. After I showed him my credentials he demanded to know my rank. I replied that C.I.C. agents were not permitted to divulge their rank. He threatened to throw me off the base. I told him that throwing me out would only make more problems for himself than thefts from his base. He had no thefts, he maintained, and he had no pilfering. I replied that he should not mind, then, answering my questions. He would not answer my questions unless I told him my rank, he said.

I was defeated. I felt that his piercing stare could see through my C.I.C. uniform to the rankless D.P. underneath. I turned on my heel and headed back to headquarters where I informed the officer of the day of the failure of my mission. Max, I was told, your mission is to get that colonel to give you his cooperation. I was assured that I had the authority to question even an American colonel, and was ordered to return immediately to his office to press my inquiry, and to call headquarters if the colonel gave me any further trouble.

At the colonel's desk I tried once more to insist that he answer my questions, but, again, without success. I called headquarters, as instructed, and ordered the colonel to take the line. What was said to him I never learned, but his face turned ashen, and when he hung up the phone he was like a pussy cat. He answered my questions in detail, and allowed me to conduct a full investigation. I no longer doubted that the C.I.C. had an effective hierachy. Organizational a hority, I was impressed to realize, reached as high as was needed.

Eventually, I was put in charge of a *Kreis*, which is similar to a small American county. In addition to other duties, I now drove regularly to my assigned *Kreis* where I worked in cooperation with the local military government and the local police on any problem arising within C.I.C. jurisdiction. As I drove my jeep back to Nürnberg one afternoon, a few large raindrops splashed down on my head. I struggled into my rain poncho as I drove rather than stopping and taking the time to yank the top up over me. The rain increased, distorting my view through the windshield. I reached forward to activate the manually-operated windshield wiper, and in so doing I swerved left and caught the soft shoulder of the road with my left front wheel. The jeep careened off the road and rolled over twice into the ditch below, coming to rest on top of me. The next thing I heard was a couple of men's voices talking above me, asking if I was alive. "Yes," I called. "Can you help me get out?"

My rescuers pushed and shoved the jeep onto its side. I crawled out and walked in a circle, checking the movements of my arms and legs, back and neck. I patted my holster frantically to make sure that my revolver was still in place. Headquarters did not gracefully accept agents' excuses for losing their hardware. The men urged me to lie down because I had a cut on my forehead, but I felt fine and persuaded the men to help me finish rolling the jeep back on its wheels. I pondered as we worked how I had managed to escape serious injury one more time, and congratulated myself on this latest proof that I had better than an average share of luck. In a jeep, the front passenger seat folds down. I had been thrown over into that seat as the jeep rolled and the seat promptly folded over me, protecting my body completely.

We got the jeep back up onto the road. The vehicle had taken the brunt of the smashup, but it started up well enough. I was able to guide the vehicle slowly back to headquarters where I filled out a flurry of forms in order to get windshield, headlamps, and fenders repaired.

An agent like myself—a voluntarily employed D.P.—was

The C.I.C.

paid very little. But we had sumptuous living quarters, good food, cars, girlfriends, half days on Saturday and all day Sunday off. Between the excitement of our daily duties and the privileges I enjoyed while impersonating an American officer, I throve on the life my friend Miles had urged me to try. It did not seem strange that I had to work the black market in order to earn the pocket money to keep up with my peers. As pseudo-officers, we were compelled to use the officers' club only. There the C.I.C. had its own table, set off from the other officers, who looked upon our rankless group with suspicion. They did not know who we were. They did not like our foreign accents. We wore their uniforms but did not fit their mold. We often ate at the officers' club and we drank there during hours of spare time. My particular addiction was Coca Cola, to which I had been introduced by the Americans soon after my liberation. I drank "Cokes" like water. At the officers' club we paid far more for our refreshments than we would have at the enlisted men's club, a place off limits to the C.I.C. As we drank and joked together, I learned the backgrounds of some of our people. There were former journalists, police officers, Americanized sons of Germans who had fled the Nazi regime, and patriots of long American lineage. One other agent and myself were the only Displaced Persons in the Nürnberg unit.

To raise pocket money, I took some of our rations of cigarettes, stockings, and soap issued to pay off informers, and traded them in the black market. The C.I.C. thought nothing of it. The black market was a Military Police problem, and one which was only arbitrarily tackled. Then I began to deal in German marks for American dollars for some of my American friends. With the commissions I made on money changing, I began to accumulate a small savings nest egg.

On summer Sundays, my friends and I took our girlfriends to the mountains. We picnicked together, then hiked off with our girls in separate directions. The Americans taught me fly-rod fishing in clear streams. We caught trout and pan-fried them on the river bank at day's end or for breakfast. No fresh fish ever tasted better.

SUMMER, 1946

From time to time during my tour of duty with the C.I.C. in Nürnberg, I took weekend trips to visit Captain Jesse Miles in Scheinfeld, a car trip of some 58 kilometers. By now, the captain had been joined by his fiancée, Ruth, whom he had met months earlier in Bad Worishöfen. I had met the captain's girlfriend there too, and so enjoyed visiting and exchanging stories with the two of them in Scheinfeld. Jesse, as I had by then been permitted to call him, also patiently answered my many questions about what life in the United States was like. I was eager to leave Europe for my new home. By midsummer, I told Jesse that I thought I had worked for the C.I.C. long enough to request their permission to go after my emigration visa in Holland. He agreed that the time was probably ripe.

I sought an interview with my superiors, presented my affidavit from Colonel Clark, and asked for a week's leave in order to seek a visa through the American Consulate in Amsterdam. I explained that I expected the Americans there could help me because I had worked for American forces instead of returning to Holland. Permission was granted, provided I travel at all times with another agent of their choosing.

An American agent I had not met before was assigned to travel with me. We were given a jeep and a leave of one week. Under no circumstances, we were warned, was I to be left in Holland. We were ordered to shoot our way out, if necessary, and to emphasize the point, we were each given an additional box of bullets for our revolvers. I was surprised at the security arrangements in my behalf, but made no comment. Perhaps all agents traveled out of territory well-armed and with companions because of the danger of being intercepted by Russian counterintelligence agents (who were known to be active also in the postwar occupation zones). Perhaps my status as a D.P.

Summer, 1946

made me particularly vulnerable to kidnap by enemy agents. Perhaps that same status made me suspect to my own C.I.C. officers. I did not know.

Once in Amsterdam, we conferred with American consular officials who looked over my papers and heard out my explanation of how I had served with U.S. forces since my release from a concentration camp. Yes, I was born in Amsterdam, Holland, I answered their query. No, I had not returned since the war to be repatriated. No, I had no family in Holland any longer. No, I had no permanent address in Amsterdam. I was a Dutch national who survived the camps, then served with American overseas forces. They shook their heads. They could not help me even though I was native born because I had not returned to Holland after the war. They suggested that I apply in Munich for a visa as a Displaced Person.

My companion and I walked silently out the consulate door. I could not obtain a visa in my native country from which I had been forcibly removed. I had struggled to stay out of the refugee camps of the disenfranchised masses called Displaced Persons. I had rebelled at having such a label pinned on me; but if accepting that label would get me a visa, then I would do it. Talking over my situation, my friend and I realized that we would have to return to Nürnberg to request permission to apply to Munich. Since we were in Amsterdam with a few days' leave, my friend—an affable fellow and interested in seeing as much as he could of Europe—agreed with me that we might as well see the town together.

I gave the American an intimate tour of Amsterdam, all the while pretending to be an American myself. When we checked in at a downtown hotel, I registered my address as Buffalo, New York, the home town of Colonel Clark. I pointed out landmarks and places of special interest as we walked and drove through the city's streets. Then even I became a tourist as we rode down the canals in tour boats, and drove out to the fishing village of Volendam where the entire community went about their daily chores in traditional costumes. We caught the ferry to the island town of Marken, another such fishing community. My family had never traveled to such provincial parts of Holland, even though the villages were close to Amsterdam. I took as much delight as the American in watching and snapping pictures of costumed natives working their boats, gardening, washing clothes, mending fish nets, tending farm animals as if the twentieth century and its wars had not touched them.

In Amsterdam, I showed my companion my old neighborhood, my school, the Miranda swimming complex, and the former homes of various relatives and friends. I avoided taking him into the old Jewish section. I made no effort to contact the Jewish community. However, we drove to the flat of my boyhood friend, Appie Klaverstyn, on the hunch that I would find him still living there. Because his parents had been of a "mixed" marriage—his mother, Jewish, his father, gentile—I thought they may well have been spared. My reasoning had been correct. Appie and his parents were at home, and an addition to the family as well, for Appie had taken a wife. We greeted one another emotionally, and I introduced my companion as an American serviceman. Our C.I.C. connections were not mentioned.

As a treat we drove the Klaverstyns out to the nearby seaside resort of Zandvoort, where our families had participated in many a holiday outing. We walked the beach and talked together through most of the afternoon. I translated from time to time for the American. Since our boyhood days, Appie had become a competent diamond polisher, a fact that surprised me since his father had not worked in the industry. I learned, however, that his grandfather and an uncle on his mother's side had both been skilled polishers. In addition, before the war, his father-in-law had been a well-known member of the diamond exchange. The Klaverstyns were still in a state of shock over the disappearance of the Jewish community, as was I, but we found few words to convey our thoughts on this painful subject. Instead, I told them about the camps I had survived and about my service with the Americans who had liberated me. I told them of my resolve to emigrate to America rather than return to Holland. Appie informed me that the queen was calling up men of our age to fight in Indonesia, and that served to confirm the wisdom of my decision to seek a new life elsewhere. In late afternoon, we drove back to town and took our leave of the Klaverstyn family.

Driving with my companion through familiar streets one afternoon, I was stopped by a traffic policeman when I tried to make a left turn from the Centuurbaan onto Van Woustraat. He began shouting at me in Dutch for violating traffic regulations. I understood him very well but shrugged my shoulders and asked him in English what I had done. He told me in Dutch that all Americans drove like wild cowboys, an image of myself that I enjoyed, but I put on a thoughtful expression and told him I did not understand. A few helpful Mokummers gathered around to assist with translations, and in this way I pretended to learn what ordinance I had violated. As my companion struggled to keep a straight face, I apologized to the officer through my interpreters for embarrassing the reputation of the American Army. The exasperated policeman sent us on our way.

We had seen enough of Amsterdam, but since we were not expected back to Nürnberg for a few more days, I suggested that we go to Antwerp, another city I could show in detail to the American. Driving to Antwerp within a few hours, we found our way to Bachelor Officers Quarters and requested meals and sleeping accommodations. Our C.I.C. credentials were inspected at the desk, and we were told to wait.

Strange, we commented to one another, that we should be asked to wait. We waited, however, for almost an hour before we asked the desk clerk if we could enter the dining room to eat while we waited. Admitted to the dining room after a backroom consultation, we were in the middle of dinner when the club C.O. introduced himself and joined us. A polite interrogation began:

"What are you boys doing in Antwerp?"
"Passing through."
"Where are you headquartered?"
"Nürnberg."

"Did you come here from Nürnberg?"
"No. We came to Amsterdam."
"What took you to Amsterdam?"
"We can't tell you that, sir."
"Why did you come to Antwerp?"
"Passing through, as we've told you. We want to see the city and Brussels as well before we return to Nürnberg."

"A likely story!" said the C.O. "As a matter of fact you cannot leave the hotel tonight, nor can you go to Brussels tomorrow. These cities are closed to unauthorized American personnel by American Military Government."

We asked on what grounds we were confined to quarters and forbidden to travel freely in Belgium, but the C.O. refused to discuss the matter. We prevailed upon him to call Nürnberg to check our story. He made the call, talking with a duty officer who confirmed that, yes, we had permission to travel to Amsterdam for a week, but, no, he did not know why we had gone to Antwerp. Why don't you ask them why they are there, he was reported to have asked.

The C.O. began to believe our story. He gave us overnight rooms; and after we cajoled him further, he gave us passes to see the town.

We spent a long night seeing Antwerp as I had never seen it as a boy. The next morning we tackled the C.O. again for passes to visit Brussels and its B.O.Q. He kidded us about wanting first a finger, then the whole hand, but he was in a better mood and eventually gave us our passes. The ice was broken enough for us to ask him about his suspicions of the day before. He told us that a full scale investigation was rumored to be in the works because of heavy thefts of military cargo in Antwerp and Brussels. When the C.O. got word that we were C.I.C. agents, he assumed that we had been sent through headquarters to start preliminary investigations. We confessed that our trip to Amsterdam had been for the purpose of seeking a visa for me, a native Dutchman, to get to the United States, and that all the other stops were as tourists as we had firmly maintained. We shook hands all around, grinning at one another, and departed.

We poked about nearby Brussels, a fine old city that I had never before visited, and spent the night without further challenge to our credentials at the local B.O.Q. The next day we drove back to Nürnberg, where we were expected by evening. There we were kidded roundly for the complete failure of our mission, and reminded that even as tourists we would have failed had we not been rescued by our headquarters.

Within a few weeks the American and I were authorized to go to Munich for another try at obtaining a visa for me. At the consular office there, we encountered the same old difficulties. No, I did not qualify as a Displaced Person because I did not live, and had never lived or registered, at a Displaced Persons camp. No, I did not qualify as a German, even though I now lived in Germany, because I was not born a German nor had I applied for citizenship. I had already learned that I did not qualify as a Dutch national, but I was just beginning to learn that by running rather than registering I had made myself a man without a country. My chances for emigration began to look doubtful, my affidavit unusable. Nobody knew what to do.

Back on duty in Nürnberg, I began to see signs and hear rumors of preparations for a big operation of some kind. At first only upper echelon agents were involved, meeting behind closed doors for long periods. Gradually, some of the rest of us were called together to start training, including an agent named Sasha, a Polish Jewish boy, also out of a concentration camp and also a Displaced Person. We received specific instructions for the part we would play in carrying out an enormous raid in the American occupation zone, the nature of which was not divulged to rank and file agents like ourselves until shortly before the raid.

Our operations as C.I.C. agents had been directed to date against Nazis and Nazi sympathizers. Now we began training to round up Communists. Such a raid had gradually reached a point of inevitability.

With the United States and Russia emerging from World War II as the two most powerful nations on earth, each ideologically opposed system presented a threat to the other. Even during the war, Churchill and Roosevelt, followed by Truman, had withheld information from the Russians. It was common knowledge that Stalin shared as little information as possible with his allies. Wrangles over occupational boundary lines and ideological control began before the last surrender treaties were signed.

The end of hostilities brought the working intelligence forces of both sides to all joint occupation areas. The Allies became as worried about communism gaining an upper hand as they were about burying fascism. The general mood was one of impatience among the Allies. Everyone had had enough of fighting, death, and deprivation. They were anxious to wind up the business of war and get back to peacetime pursuits.

Russian Communist agents were known to swarm the occupation zones, engaging in intelligence gathering and the recruitment of sympathizers. We C.I.C. agents were not surprised to be informed, then, that a great counter-intelligence raid was in the offing. Many of us welcomed the opportunity to take part in an action designed to reduce communist influence in Europe. I shared the belief that communism would be as disastrous for free men as fascism had been.

The Saturday evening of the raid, all agents were called together and given a broad outline of what the evening held in store and what our particular duties would be. It was then we learned that the purpose of the raid was to pull in Communists and Communist sympathizers. Wearing our uniforms and fully equipped from handcuffs to handguns, we drove our cars and jeeps to a 10 PM rendezvous at the Nürnberg stadium Hitler had once used for his rallies. We arrived to find the stadium half filled with military police and GI's, none of whom were aware of the nature of this action. Over the loudspeaker system the leaders announced that the C.I.C., with the cooperation of the armed forces and the military police, would lead a raid shortly after midnight throughout the American zone.

Summer, 1946

Simultaneous raids, we were told, would be carried out in every major city of the British and French occupation zones under the leadership of their counterintelligence units. We were to travel in teams to make our arrests. Each jeep or car would carry four men: a C.I.C. agent, a military policemen, and two GI's. We were to proceed swiftly and silently with the intent of taking our victims by surprise. Those arrested were to be escorted to strategically parked roundup trucks. They were not to be roughed up unless resistance made such action necessary.

Just before midnight departure, our team assignments were distributed. My team was responsible for bringing in a small number of suspects, listed in order of the arrests to be made. Their names, streets, and apartment numbers, conditions to expect, and positions of gathering trucks, were spelled out. Photographs were attached.

We broke quietly into apartment houses, sneaked up flights of stairs, kicked in doors, and tried to overpower our victims before they could fully awaken. Some had guns, but we gave them no chance to use them. We picked up both men and women, sometimes whole families, encountering little resistance. Once postively identified, our suspects were taken to the designated trucks, after which they were driven to interrogation centers. The roundup raids continued all night and through most of Sunday.

At the centers interrogating teams systematically questioned all those suspects fingered by counterintelligence. Some were released. Many were detained in jails. Interrogations and reports took up the rest of the week. My duties ended after the roundup, however, and we raiders could catch up on our sleep. There was little else for us to do.

A superior had given me a permanent pass to the Nürnberg war crimes trials, assuming that the trials would interest me. At the time, however, I did not have enough perspective on the trials to want to attend and learn from them. I had been fed (unsuccessfully) into the Nazi extermination machine as into a meat grinder because I was a Jew. There had been no justice in what had happened to me. I had little appetite now for attending formal trials which were settling degrees of guilt on the madmen responsible. I wanted to get on with my life, to continue trying new experiences, to forget the past. Crying over wrongs and nursing revenge would bring back only bitter memories of that past, a past I wanted to put behind me. The words of the Polish prisoner I had met in Buna still echoed in my mind: Forget your past. Forget you ever had a family. Find out how this place works and learn to survive in it. Live for tomorrow.

Nevertheless, I attended a couple of sessions of the trials during the quiet days following our raid. I looked into the faces of some former high Nazi officials—faces and names I can no longer recall with assurance—and listened to accusations, rhetoric, and explanations. The courtroom scene was like a pretentious stage play in which the players debated in lofty terms some moral problems of war. I must have been through a different war. I had not been a pawn on a grand chess board. I knew who had hunted me down, thrown me behind barbed wire, and taught me to survive on terms I would rather forget. The Nazis had buried Jews with enthusiam and laughed with satisfaction at the moral reduction of those who tried for survival on their terms. When my associates asked me what I thought of the trials, I told them the truth: I did not know what to think. I did not understand why these trials were necessary. It was obvious to me that the whole bunch was guilty.

Suddenly my superiors became concerned about the well-being of Sasha—the one other Displaced Person in our unit—and myself. They realized that as Displaced Persons the two of us were in great danger of being picked up by Russian counterintelligence agents. The Russians were in Nürnberg for the trials, along with the British, French, and Americans, and their cadre of counterintelligence people were known to be out for blood over our raid. It was assumed they possessed lists of our names and backgrounds. As D.P.'s Sasha and I could disappear overnight, and no one would have the power to do anything about it.

The C.I.C. decided it was time to intervene in our behalf

in the matter of obtaining visas. They could have turned their heads and let us disappear with very few people being the wiser. They chose to honor their initial promises to look after us, a trait I had learned to respect greatly in the Americans. In the first days of September, Sasha, who also had a sponsor's affidavit, and I were sent to Frankfurt, where C.I.C. main headquarters were situated, as well as those of the U.S. Army and the State Department. We were assigned rooms in a C.I.C.-maintained hotel, and advised for our own safety to confine ourselves to the hotel except for escorted trips on official business.

At headquarters, a legal officer examined our papers and interviewed us at length. He then took our cases himself before State Department representatives. Papers were signed and stamped, and we were quickly cleared but for our medical examinations. At the hospital where we were examined, my rising hopes were almost dashed again when I was told that my chest X-ray revealed TB scarring, and that a more detailed set of X-rays would have to be taken. Technicians took more X-rays and sent me back to my hotel to sweat out news of the results until the next day. Calling in the morning, as instructed, I learned the last hurdle was behind me. There was no evidence of live TB.

Within twenty-four hours, Washington sent through our visa numbers. We were cleared to emigrate. Our visas would be ready to pick up the following week. The legal officer put us in touch with the U.S. Transportation Agency to arrange for our passage on the earliest available ship for the United States.

SEPTEMBER, 1946

From Frankfurt, Sasha and I were flown back to Nürnberg on a C-47 bucket seat cargo plane. Taking off on my first flight, I sweated with anxiety until we were airborne, then thrilled to the sight of towns and rolling farmlands unfolding beneath us.

At our headquarters everyone gathered to congratulate us over our good fortune. We had a week in which to wind up our affairs. The U.S. Transportation Agency notified us that we were booked for passage on the S.S. Ernie Pyle out of Bremerhaven on September 19, and that we each owed $142 for our tickets. To insure our safety, agents escorted us on our errands about town. We arranged to draw the monies to pay our ship passage. We visited a tailor who turned out inexpensive suits for us within a few days. Each night a different agent hosted a party in our behalf.

Sasha and I flew back to Frankfurt for the completion of paperwork at the State Department. The process took several days, and during that time we stayed once again at the C.I.C. hotel. With visas and official photographs finally in our possession, we were flown to Bremen and confined to rooms in C.I.C. quarters to await the departure date of our ship.

On the morning of September 19, we were driven to Bremerhaven and turned over to the captain of the S.S. Ernie Pyle, a converted liberty ship. The captain was instructed to keep us on board in all European ports. Sasha and I stood at the rail and watched expectantly as people began to board. We sailed to Le Havre, a trip of two days, and picked up more passengers. Except for a few of us, the ship filled up with American repatriates, people who had been caught overseas for one reason or another when the war broke out. More than a year after the war was over, these Americans were just being readmitted after lengthy checking and clearance procedures. Once the last passenger had boarded, the captain ordered the anchor hoisted, and our voyage began. The ship steered through the choppy waters of the English channel into the vast Atlantic where the waters were no calmer.

Little by little Sasha and I parted company after we hit the open sea. We had not worked together or spent time in one another's company until after the big counterintelligence raid in Nürnberg. We had not developed a close relationship and felt no obligation to stick together as immigrants. Our small liberty ship teemed with Americans speaking European languages; indeed, they seemed to have forgotten their own. Communicating in one language or another, I found shipboard acquaintances easy to make. The ship itself was crowded and uncomfortable. To make matters worse, we ran into a storm almost immediately. As the Ernie Pyle tossed and plunged, most passengers succumbed to seasickness. They took to their bunks in the hold and mingled their helpless groans with the creaks and groans of the ship.

The hold began to smell so badly from vomit that I could not make myself climb down into it. A number of passengers felt as I did that the deck was preferable. On top we could better keep our equilibrium and breathe lungsful of fresh air. In spite of the storm the September winds were warm. A small group of us claimed an abandoned gun platform from which the wartime artillery had been removed. We dragged our mattresses up from the hold and placed them under the shelter of the gun platform. Some of the girls in the group obligingly consented to run up and downstairs for sandwiches and other supplies. The storm did not let up, and even on the deck most of us felt seasick. When someone reported that the crew had a supply of cognac they were willing to sell, we began to buy and drink the stuff with the idea of half-anesthetizing ourselves. The storm raged and the little ship plunged until the day before we approached New York. We continued to drink, loll about glassy-eyed, and occasionally run to the rail to vomit.

On a calm and glorious rainy evening, the loudspeaker announced that New York harbor was just becoming visible. Passengers poured onto the deck to watch the Statue of Liberty come into view. We dropped anchor at the entrance to the harbor, and many of us stared in awe until darkness obliiterated our view of the Statue of Liberty.

I peered with grateful humility at the symbol of LIBERTY in New York harbor. Liberty. I stood at the gates of the nation that dared to welcome the downtrodden of the world to a haven of freedom and promise. For months I had imagined the day when I would see this statue. It meant I was going to find my way as a free man among the most remarkable people on earth. I wanted to become an American citizen as soon as I was able. I believed, too, that America stood waiting to compensate me with her caring people and her wealth for much that I had lost. Painful memories would no longer creep into my sleeping and waking hours. I would stand tall and make myself worthy of America. I wished that my parents could see me. Here was their son, Max Rodriguez Garcia—to whom they had granted life many times over by their actions and teachings—arrived at the land of liberty. They would have shared my gratitude.

Here, also, stood Max Garcia who had pledged to himself that when he set foot on American soil, he would forsake his Jewish identity. I had reasoned that Jewish heritage was too perilous a condition to chain myself to any longer. I had barely escaped with my life for the indiscretion of having been born a Jew, and I was no longer willing to subject myself to the unpredictable burdens of such a heritage.

Another Max Garcia stared at the statue as well: a studied copy of an American GI, confident, tough, and looking forward to conquering on the homefront as he had abroad. The cars, the privileges, the power I had acquired as a C.I.C. agent were not far behind me. I could hardly wait to see what America itself held in store for me.

Early the next morning I pulled myself together and forced myself to go below deck to clean up. I was a sorry specimen and I knew it. The army uniform I had worn throughout the voyage was filthy. My body reeked and my face bristled with stubble. I was anxious to clean myself up. I felt like a groom readying himself for his bride. I wanted to make myself as presentable as possible to my new country. I showered, shaved, brushed my teeth, and put on a fresh army shirt and my new suit of ersatz fabric. Feeling wonderfully expectant, I charged up to the deck to watch the dawn gather strength over calm waters.

The harbor pilot boarded to help guide the Ernie Pyle through the harbor. I stood among acquaintances on the foredeck as the ship glided silently past the Statue of Liberty and an enormous banner which read,"WELCOME HOME, WELL DONE." A morning fog bank obliterated all but the tops of the New York skyline. Buildings taller than I had ever seen penetrated a high white fog mass beneath them. We passengers passed the cognac bottle for the last time and wished one another well.

I wiped away tears of gratitude as the boat docked on September 30, 1946. I went through immigration in a turmoil of anticipation, searching the waiting crowd for the face of Colonel Clark. But as officials finished checking my papers, a woman called for me. She introduced herself as a representative of the Travelers Aid Society, and explained that Colonel Clark had arranged for the agency to meet and assist me until I could be put on a train to Buffalo that afternoon. He had sent the money for a coach ticket.

I thanked the Travelers Aid woman and followed her, swallowing my overwhelming disappointment that Colonel Clark had not come to meet me. I knew that I was in New York and that the town of Buffalo was in New York, and I could not understand why he could not have taken the time out to meet my ship. It was not until I completed the long train journey to Buffalo and was met in the early hours of morning by Arthur Clark, husband to Jean, and father of two small girls, that I began to realize how far Buffalo was and how tied down was Colonel Clark. The train ride out of Grand Central Station had been comfortable to the point of luxury for a European boy who expected coach-car seats to be upright wooden benches but who was ushered, instead, to a cushioned and upholstered seat with an adjustable back. I talked easily with some homeward-bound GI's taking the same train. Occasionally we ducked into the men's room to share whiskey and water in paper cups and laugh over army reminiscences. We had come through the war and were going home—a good feeling. I, Max Garcia, was also going home.

Around 2 AM I stepped off the train at the Buffalo station to find the Clarks waiting for me. The Colonel was wearing civilian clothes, a real shock for me, but otherwise he looked as I had remembered him, tall and wearing that shy smile of his. He introduced his pretty young wife, not many years older than I, and asked that I call them Jean and Arthur. Arthur, at that time, was 31 years old. The ride out to Snyder, the suburb where they lived, was long. I told them excitedly about the C.I.C. getting me to America in a month's time, about my seasick days on a storm-tossed liberty ship, about my glance at New York buildings, the kindness of Travelers Aid, the pleasantness of American train coaches. We did not talk long when we reached the house. Jean showed me to the tidy bedroom they had fixed up for me, and we all went to bed.

Had my life been a movie such as I was used to watching, the film probably would have ended here: after many hardships, the orphaned boy finds a family, is welcomed to the land of his dreams, and lives happily ever after. Instead, I awoke in the morning to a continuation of my life and its accumulating collection of problems, not the least of which was the wide difference between my expectations and the realities that faced me.

PART 5

THE IMMIGRANT

1946—1947

In the morning, Jean introduced me to the Clarks' two wide-eyed little girls. Lynda was five years old. Barbara was two. Jean showed me around the spacious, well-furnished rooms of their home, then took me outside. The house was one of a block of solid residences centered on well-tended lawns and fronting on a wide, tree-lined avenue. They owned a Canadian summer home as well, Jean told me, with a beach front on Lake Erie.

The Clarks took me to visit both of their sets of parents, all longtime Buffalo residents. The senior Clarks lived on the ground floor of an even larger house than their children's, on a wider street, and in an older but elegant residential area. Jean's family lived in a fine home nearby. I was a long way from home. Even the wealthiest members of my large Amsterdam family had not owned homes. Buying a home was a goal none of our tribe had ever dared to contemplate, but for Americans owning a home appeared to be the norm.

While I was with the C.I.C., I had sent my savings (black market earnings) to Buffalo, and Arthur had opened a small savings acount in my name. It was from this account that Colonel Clark had forwarded a money order to cover the cost of my ship passage. A few dollars remained in the account, and Arthur suggested that we use them to shop for some new clothes. Except for my suit, my few belongings were army-issue, including my shoes. Arthur drove me downtown and through the heavy traffic of the city's center core. My GI friends had not been exaggerating. Every family in America seemed to own a car. We shopped in enormous department stores through great stocks of clothing. I could not stop staring as we walked from one amazing emporium to another. Arthur advised me about style as we selected shirts, slacks, underwear, socks and shoes. By late afternoon, I was dressed in my new clothes, and proud to think I looked as American as anyone passing me on the street.

Within a few days, Arthur Clark took me on a tour of his father's small chemical plant, in which he was a partner. After dinner one evening thereafter, he encouraged me to discuss with him my plans for the future. I told Arthur I thought I should enlist in the army right away because of a law still in effect that gave immigrants the right to full citizenship within 90 days if they enlisted in the army. In that way, I explained, I would have the advantage of citizenship within a short time, and I could serve in work familiar to me while I got used to American ways. I would then be in a better position to decide what to do next.

Arthur would not hear of it. I had never tried civilian life, he pointed out, and he thought it was important that I learn to get along as a free man in an unregulated society.

I could not tell him, because I could hardly grasp it myself, that I was becoming frightened at the concept of such freedom, and even more so of finding my way in a classless society. I had been raised to understand the limited horizons of the European workingman. Even in the army, I had noticed, the sons of American plumbers, factory laborers, small grocery-store owners, were well-off—some even rich—by my standards. They had showed me pictures of their homes, their cars, their bathing-suited girlfriends, and told me their plans for going on to college and interesting careers when they got home. I greatly admired my American friends' bold confidence that the future was theirs; but for myself, secretly, I had no such confidence. How was I going to transform myself from an unschooled workingman to a trained professional such as I dreamed of becoming?

Nevertheless, since Arthur wanted to hear about aspirations, I told him that I had not given up on my idea of one day becoming an architect, but that I did not know how to go about financing my education. Arthur told me I could work to be anything I wanted, but that his help would stop short of underwriting my education as he had children of his own to bring up and educate. What he did propose, to fulfill his sponsorship pledge to keep me off the welfare rolls for five years or until I got my citizenship, was to give me a job in his chemical plant, and to stand behind me with whatever help and advice I needed. He hoped for the sake of my development that I would choose to start there rather than in the army.

I had not known what to expect, but I was learning. I had not come to America to work in a factory, not even Arthur's. If he saw this as a first step to a larger experience, I did not. I believed that to work in a factory was to accept a ticket to stay in the working class. If Arthur was being generous in discouraging me from entering the army, receiving quick citizenship and a quick end to his responsibilities, I did not realize it. I had been given so much by the Americans in Europe after my liberation—cars, prestige, ready access to things I wanted—that it had not occurred to me that I might have to start out with less in the homeland itself.

Right from the start, I resented the factory job. I worked in a packing line with a number of girls who had been employed there for some time. When I discovered that I was being paid more than they, even though less skilled, I resented that too. The unfairness of it! We sealed domestic chemicals in commercial wrappers as they came down a conveyor belt, then packed the finished products in boxes. The girls chatted about their friends and their problems. I was an outsider with foreign ways and a foreign accent.

I had arrived in the country a cocky youth full of dreams of instant successes. In the factory, I soon grew unsure of myself, and hesitant about speaking. At the Clark's home, Jean shrank from my company. She found my manners crude and my army-learned English, coarse. Arthur advised me to improve my manners and my language, even to attend night school in English, because Jean was concerned for the sake of the children about my many crudities and the coarseness of my language. I became even more shy of people and withdrawn, but hostile in conduct. An ungrateful employee, I was also a problematical grown son to an already burdened young mother of two small children. The Clarks and I were crowding one another. Within a few weeks I took a small room by myself close to the downtown area and my factory job. The Clarks invited me to take Sunday dinners with them in order to stay in touch.

The nights were lonely. The factory job went no better. The migraine headaches I had experienced from time to time since boyhood, returned. One day I walked into Arthur's office and told him I was quitting, that I could no longer work on an assembly line. I thought him unfair to pay me more than his better-skilled girls. Arthur reminded me that he had promised to back me up financially until I became a citizen and that the factory job was his way of doing so. He had hoped that I would save my money and that within a few years I could be off to a good start in whatever direction I wanted to go. I told him not to worry about me, that I could take care of myself.

I landed a job for the Christmas season in the toy department of Adam, Meldrum, & Anderson, a large Buffalo department store. There I worked in a fairyland of toys, and enjoyed playing with the hottest selling item of that season, a little machine that melted down various colored plastics for pouring into a variety of design molds. The job was much more to my liking than the assembly line. I began to open up to people again, to joke and enjoy myself. An assistant buyer invited me to his home for my first family Thanksgiving in America. Wherever I went, I listened well and tried to improve my vocabulary. I imitated the American way of speaking, trying hard to lose my Dutch accent.

In January the Christmas season job ended. I became a busboy at the Statler Hotel, working from 4 PM to 1 AM, setting and clearing tables, replenishing water and ice in glasses, and so on. Dinner was included as part of my salary. I moved to rooms at a nearby YMCA so that I had only a short walk to my job.

The winter of 1947 was bitter cold and, to hear everyone talk, it was typical. The winds blew in from the north and from across the Great Lakes bringing with them more snow than I had ever seen in one place. Walls of snow so high I could not see over them rose beside the shoveled sidewalks around the hotel. Arthur, to whom I still talked occasionally, urged me to get out and participate in winter sports, reminding me of the stories I had once told him about ice-skating on Amsterdam canals. But I no longer felt like a boy in a mood to play, and was not inclined to set foot outside except to walk to work or to necessary errands. If Arthur wondered what had become of his one-time resourceful aide to the 319th, I wondered how to fit into American society. What I knew about surviving, Americans knew about playing. They turned every season into a celebration complete with appropriate sports and family gift-giving holidays. Everyone had a house, a car, and sporting equipment for each season. I looked on but did not know how to join the party.

Because of my night work and the bitterness of the weather, I spent most of my days at the movies, feeding my dreams, staying warm. I worked every night but one, and on Saturdays and Sundays. This, too, filled me with resentment for I had the strange idea that Americans should not have to work on Saturdays and Sundays. I was fed up enough to quit my flunky job with its long night hours, but I soon was forced to take a similar one. I became a short-order cook at a White Tower diner, grilling hamburgers and eggs on the night shift from 10 PM to 6 AM.

I bought New York City newspapers and began planning to move there, where I assumed I could fairly easily find a job as an interpreter, perhaps in the export-import business. I did not tell the Clarks about my plans but saved my salary until I could afford a bus ticket.

I was probably an exceptional immigrant Jew to arrive in New York and make no effort to contact its Jewish communities. I checked in at a "Y", took a room, and began tramping the streets in search of a job. In a day or two it became apparent that I was not educationally qualified for an interpreting job, or, in fact, for any job I went after. The busy streets and towering, cold buildings were intimidating. My money dwindled alarmingly. No one spoke to me except to transact business, and I grew desperate. Finally, I was accepted for a job—that of a door-to-door magazine salesman.

Four or five of us salesmen were driven daily to New Jersey, where each of us was assigned to a sales area of a few city blocks. You're a natural, the boss had told me. Just tell your prisoner story and you'll sell hundreds of magazines and earn big commissions.

For weeks I trudged up apartment steps and tried to get at least a foot in the door by starting my story. I did not sell many magazines but I learned that there were some very lonely American housewives. Sometimes women responded to my sincerely-spoken story with seductive smiles, but no subscription. Some even opened up their robes to reveal parts of their naked bodies. With each such incident I fled in confusion, ignoring the advice of my co-workers: "If they want it, give it. You'll get bigger commissions, idiot, and some fun besides." I quit, demanded to be paid off, and was left stranded somewhere in New Jersey.

I was a beaten man. For a young immigrant in a hurry, America had turned out to be a cold, inhospitable country where my efforts were answered with indifference. My thoughts went back to Europe, to people and customs I understood. I looked at the money in my hand and took the bus to the nearest big city, Philadelphia. There I spent the night in the bus station. In the morning I went to the recruiting office and signed up for 18 months with the United States Army. I called Arthur Clark to tell him of my enlistment. He pleaded with me to come back to Buffalo and to try to work things out there. Much as before, I explained that I needed to join the army because I was familiar with army life and because I hoped it would help me prepare to live in the United States. I could not yet cope with living and working by myself. I think Arthur began to understand how I felt. He wished me luck, and told me to stay in touch, words of friendship that I badly needed.

I was inducted on March 10, 1947, and sent to Fort Jackson, just outside of Columbia, South Carolina. The spring weather was hot and humid as I started basic training in a Southern army camp. The wartime law granting citizenship after 90 days to immigrant enlisted men had expired at the end of December, 1946.

1947—1948

As I started my enlistment in 1947, nearly everyone who had served in World War II was getting out of the army. There was little glory in joining up. The honors and the thrills were gone. The only veterans left were those who had decided to make a career of military service. Men who had become ranking officers during the war now took reductions in rank in order to stay in the service. A captain, for instance, would accept downgrading to master sergeant, a master sergeant to buck sergeant.

Central South Carolina, where I was stationed, was not at all like upstate New York where I had lived during my first months in the United States. The climate was hotter and people seemed to live closer to the land. South Carolinians moved slowly and spoke in a drawling accent that I often strained to understand. They ate a different diet from the Northerners. Their towns held little of interest for an Amsterdam-born GI who was stationed among them.

To my amazement, Southerners followed strict rules for the separation of black and white citizens that I had not observed in the North. In the towns, blacks had to drink from separate and designated fountains, use separate public bathrooms, eat in separate restaurants, take seats in the back of public buses. In Columbia, the capital of South Carolina, there was an unwritten understanding that no blacks were to be seen on the streets after dark. I had not thought it possible that in the United States some of its citizens could be discriminated against much as we Jews had been under early Nazi occupation. I asked around, incredulous, and learned that discriminatory policies against blacks were standard practice in the Southern states.

At Fort Jackson, I began eight weeks of basic training in a company of young recruits; but, unlike the recruits, I already understood army life. The war-trained buck sergeants understood me too. They knew where I had come from and that I was a war veteran of sorts who had never taken basic training. I trained and exercized no more than I had to. I produced my old camera and requested permission to become company photographer. The sergeants allowed it. When we were ordered to the parade ground, I could often be found on the sidelines taking pictures of our company in action. I could also wangle a pass to Columbia (where I found nothing to do) when my fellow recruits were confined to the base. In just such ways I took up my comfortable old game of wheeling and dealing to try to improve my position.

As basic training neared an end, the recruits were allowed to choose a school for further military training. I requested C.I.C. school with one goal in mind: I wanted an overseas assignment. I was homesick for Europe. In America, I did not "belong" in the same way I had belonged with American troops overseas. I had looked around and thought until my brain ached about what I might do to make a place for myself in the new country. I had to admit defeat. I was lonely, and longed to be back among people, customs, and idioms I understood. I had little in common with the beer-drinking, comic-book-reading American kids who made up our company.

In order to qualify for C.I.C. school, I passed a battery of tests. I was notified of my eligibility except for one requirement. I had to be a citizen. My request for C.I.C.

school was denied. My alternate request for training at the Military Police School of the Criminal Investigation Division was granted.

The C.I.D. Military Police School was at Carlisle Barracks, near Gettysburg, Pennsylvania. Once a cavalry school, Carlisle Barracks was a pleasant old army post of brick buildings set amoung rolling green hills. As a lone private amoung corporals and sergeants, I attended daily classes for more than a month. Near the end of our training, rumors began to circulate that our whole graduating class was to be sent to Germany. I was elated, and went about my routines in good spirits. We were ordered to undergo physical and dental check-ups preliminary to our being sent overseas. The physical was no problem, but I steeled myself for what was to be my second encounter with a dentist since my attendance at the middle school in Antwerp. Dating from that time, I had a phobic fear of dentists and the pain they caused. My teeth were in poor shape, badly out of line and riddled with cavities. They gave me problems I preferred to deal with by closing my mouth and thinking about something else. Submitting to a dentist had long been on my list of situations to avoid; but, if I were to get overseas, I had no choice.

The young army dentist who ordered me to open up so that he could have a look, poked about my mouth for some time, then lifted one foot onto my chair, leaned an elbow on his knee, and let me have it:

"You hate dentists, don't you, soldier."

"Yes, sir."

"Well, your luck has run out. We're going to pull six teeth and fix up a number of cavities."

I had already thought of a way out of this predicament. "If you don't mind, sir, I'd rather go downtown to have my teeth fixed by an experienced private dentist. I understand they will use general anesthesia if I request it."

I recognized the young dental officer as Jewish, and, perhaps he saw that I, too, was Jewish. I made no sign, but when he began to argue with me about the stupidity of neglecting my teeth, then wanting to pay a private dentist from my meager wages when he could do the same work for me without charge, I began to have confidence in him. He told me that the use of novocaine, a local anesthesia, was standard dental practice in the army, and that it would be effective. I let him shoot my mouth full of novocaine and accomplish all the yanking and drilling work he considered necessary. The work required several sessions, and submitting to it took as much courage as I could summon, courage I would have lacked had I not instinctively liked the dentist, or had I thought for one minute that I would not be sent overseas.

In July of 1947, our class graduated and received orders to prepare to ship out to Germany. Two nights before we were to leave a telegram came informing me that I was excluded from the shipping list. No reason was given. When my classmates pulled out, I was still in Carlisle Barracks, a bitterly disappointed recruit, awaiting stateside reassignment.

I was sent to Fort Lee, Virginia, to serve in a special C.I.D. detachment. There I pulled duty for less than a week when I was ordered to transfer out of the C.I.D. detachment and into the regular military police. Reason given: I was not a citizen.

Assigned as a guard to the towers of a prisoner stockade, I stood watch in rotation with others. I paced about the towers while the prisoners paced in the compound below. Sleep came hard during my hours off duty. When I dozed, I slept fitfully, sometimes awakening to my own screams, my body soaked with sweat. The hours I served on duty were stretches of gloomy introspection. My off-duty hours were spent alone. I refused the invitations of other M.P.'s to join them on their weekend trips to town. My bunkmates eventually complained that I screamed in my sleep and was so restless no one else could sleep. I was sent to a camp doctor, who listened to my history and examined me, then sent me to three other doctors, one after another, whose specialties I did not know. As a result of their consultations, I was relieved of guard duty on the stockade towers. My commanding officer had been advised that my history as a concentration camp prisoner made me a potential threat to prisoners in the stockade and others because of the possiblity of my acting out problems of reversed identity.

New orders were cut for me, and I was assigned to a base in Maryland. No sooner did I arrive there than I was told to put in for a transfer. Reason given: I was not a citizen. In this instance, lo and behold, the army had assigned me to a top-secret base. Until my transfer could be arranged, the security officer gave me a colored tag and assigned me to a barracks block with others who were awaiting transfer or discharge.

The base was a coding and decoding center that served the entire East Coast. Everyone wore color-coded tags and identification photographs around their necks. Free movement and talk about one's work were not permitted. Individuals passed from one area to another only according to the color of the tags they wore. There was absolutely nothing for me to do. The camp was situated in the country, well away from main roads. I sat around for a week before I approached a sergeant and begged him for work of some kind so that I would not go out of my mind. The sergeant thought about my request, then suggested that I take duty on a supply truck that ran between their camp and Camp Belvoir, Virginia, to pick up rations. I went out on the supply truck about three times a week. The rest of the time I played cards or chess, and went to every movie shown on the base.

Weeks went by and still there were no new orders. I requested a weekend pass to Washington, D.C. The C.O. mulled the idea over for awhile because I was not a permanent member of the camp, but he finally consented to issue me regular weekend passes to Washington. Thus I became acquainted with the capital city, toured the federal buildings, congressional chambers, and other points of interest, like any tourist. I also met hostesses at the U.S.O. there, and began to spend most of my weekend time at the servicemen's club, socializing, dancing, consuming refreshments.

After two and a half months I was still frittering away time on that post, weekending in Washington. At the

U.S.O. one weekend I met and talked at length with a GI who worked in the Army Medical Library in Washington. He learned that I could speak and read a few European languages. When he heard that I was a soldier in search of an assignment, he encouraged me to try to get into the Medical Library, where, he assured me, linguists were badly needed. His description of duty at the library was inviting, and the idea of working in Washington appealed to me.

When I returned to camp, I finished my usual Monday-morning supply truck duty before trotting off to the administration building to tackle a sergeant on the subject of my transfer.

"Sir," I said, "I have a lead on a translating job with the Army Medical Library in Washington. Since I am not wanted on this base but have no other orders, I would like to request a three-day pass in mid-week to follow up that job lead."

The sergeant stared at me. "Garcia, do you know you can't do that? You can't just go out looking for a job in the army. The job has to come to you, very properly, with orders."

"Yes, sir, but look what's happened to me with all these proper orders. I keep getting assigned to bases where the army can't use me because I'm not a citizen. I'm trying to tell you that I've found a division of the army that could use my training, citizen or not."

"You'll have to wait, Garcia," said the sergeant. "I'm sure your orders are on the way, and reassignment is not far off."

After a few more weeks without orders I returned to the sergeant in a desperate mood. This time I persuaded him to approach a lieutenant with me about trying for the library post in Washington. Together we went through a similar routine with the lieutenant that I had already been through with the sergeant. Eventually, however, the lieutenant saw the logic of my request. "Okay," he agreed, "Let's give the soldier a three-day pass and see what happens. Maybe he can get himself reassigned by his own efforts. We sure as hell haven't been successful at it."

I went to Washington, and to the Army Medical Library on Constitution Avenue next to the Smithsonian Institute. My friend, when I found him, took me immediately to the commanding officer, a captain. I discussed with him my qualifications for a translator-clerk job with the library, and briefed him fully on my present predicament. The captain took up his phone and called someone, apparently on a high level, giving him my serial number and asking that I be transferred to the medical library. He said he would wait by his phone for an answer, and hung up. We talked about the nature of the work I would be expected to do, and waited for the phone to ring. A return call came within a half an hour and cleared me to transfer, as requested. The captain told me to go back to camp and wait for orders.

At the base, my story that I had successfully managed my own reassignment was met with good-natured skepticism. I sweated out a week and a half more of waiting, then had the satisfaction of receiving orders for transfer to the Army Medical Library.

The library was a plum of a job. The usual army routines were absent. I worked in the reference division with a small detachment of about ten men, learning clerking duties, translating title sheets of foreign books into English, assisting civilians who drifted in and out. I worked, too, on translations of captured German documents.

Because we had no base, we got "rations and quarters," that is, we received monthly pay plus a weekly allowance for food and lodgings. Most of us rented cheap rooms and were able to save a little of our food and lodging money. There was no reveille. There were no inspections. I lived in a Northwest Washington boarding house where I took two meals a day, seven days a week. I met my fellow boarders, many of them students at George Washington University nearby. A little at a time, I bought some civilian clothing to wear weekends when we were off duty. My life warmed up.

Acquainting myself with university students, most of whom were younger and seemed no smarter than I, I began to realize that college might not be out of the question, particularly as I had enlisted under the "GI Bill", which extended educational benefits to servicemen based on length of service. I enrolled in the U.S. Armed Forces Institute and started night high school equivalency classes toward a high school diploma.

In the spring of 1948, I was offered the rank of corporal in the Army Medical Department with the stipulation that I reenlist for another two years. I would be a buck sergeant within three years, I was promised. But I turned down the inducement to stay in the service beyond my current term.

My library work among educated GI's, my association with university students, my high school studies—all served to give me confidence that I could seek a higher level of education. I wanted out of the army and into college.

1948—1953

On September 10, 1948, exactly 18 months after I had enlisted, I took my discharge from the army as a private, first class. Five days later I received my high school equivalency diploma, just in time to begin fall classes at George Washington University under the full benefits of the GI Bill.

College classes, I discovered, were challenging and enjoyable; and the open life style of a large city university, agreeable. I looked forward to studying for and attending my classes. In my spare time I tried out some of the school's clubs and social activities. Soon I was part of a small group of friends with similar interests, and three of us became close.

One friend got me a bid to his national fraternity, which allowed neither Jews nor Negroes among its members. I could not duck away from experiencing deep humiliation when I learned of that policy, but such humiliations had long been a fact of my survival. I became a pledge, only to drop out soon afterwards, not (consciously) because of policies of discrimination, but (as I told my fraternity friends) because I learned how high the dues were. Fraternity life was not for students like me, nor the taking to heart of racist attitudes, remarks, and policies that wove through our daily lives like a game or a threat, depending upon who the player was.

Between classes I spent most of my spare time playing bridge in the student union lounge with my two new friends, Jim Pearce, a Floridian, and Budge Beckman, an upstate New Yorker. That year the three of us went to Budge's home in Westfield, New York, for Thanksgiving, and to Jim's home in St. Petersburg, Florida, for Christmas. Both families welcomed me warmly and treated me as openly and casually as if I were another son. From then on, I was assured of a home to go to during school vacations.

I became an avid student of American history and government. Under an excellent teacher, I learned about key figures, acts, and documents representing almost two hundred years of governmental policy. I studied eagerly the functions and mechanics of the three branches of American government, and decided that American participatory democracy was far more effective than the social democracy of my early political training. I often sought out my professor after class because he always answered in detail the many questions I posed to him. I finally asked his advice about how I might get started in architectural training. He told me that I was headed in the right direction to be an undergraduate in general studies, but that I should soon enroll in an architectural school. Stick with it, he said, even knowing you will have to work most of your way through. As to where I should settle down, he emphasized that if I wanted to understand the many-faceted character of the United States, I should get away from the Eastern seaboard. He believed that the East was too dominated by European thought to understand the strong influence of other vast regions of the country. Far too many immigrants, he thought, stagnated in New York and other large Eastern cities because they were afraid to break their ties with Europe. Like Horace Greeley, he advised me to go West. There, he said, I would find not only an opportunity to develop myself, but to help influence the direction of this still-growing country.

George Washington offered no architecture course other than a survey history course in the fine arts department. This I took in my first term. I covered the curriculum offered and supplemented my studies by joining the art club, then becoming its president. After the Christmas recess I continued a full schedule of classes at George Washington, but I also enrolled in a class in residential design at an adult night school. Our instructor was a young Washington architect named Nick Satterlee (now deceased), who struggled to teach a class of do-it-yourself house builders some of the elementary points of good residential design. I was the only real student of architecture in the class, and Nick seemed glad to have me there. He offered me babysitting work at his Georgetown home, which he had recently remodeled, encouraging me to browse through his extensive architectural library whenever I "sat" with his two little girls. By spring I asked Nick what he thought of my attending architecture school full time. He not only encouraged me, but used his influence with an old friend who had become the dean of a new architectural college at North Carolina State University to get me accepted for the fall, 1949, term. He also recommended me for a summer job with an up-and-coming Washington architect named Vernon de Mars. Vernon—who later developed an outstanding practice in California—taught me the rudiments of drafting, including some valuable lessons in holding pencil leads to achieve various line qualities.

At North Carolina State University in Raleigh, I immersed myself in architecture, working often more than fifteen hours a day at classwork and design problems. I studied eagerly under excellent instructors. My favorite design teacher was Mrs. Nowicki, a Polish architect married to Matthew Nowicki, another Polish architect, who had recently collaborated with LeCorbusier on the United Nations headquarters building in New York. Mr. Nowicki also taught us at intervals. Frank Lloyd Wright and Buckminster Fuller came through Raleigh to lead annual seminars. I managed to hear Mr. Wright during my first year when I joined a group of freshman architecture students who "crashed" a Wright party for more advanced students. We were permitted to stay only by the intervention of the great man himself. I had first rate instruction from teachers near my own age, such as George Matsumoto, now a distinguished California architect.

Through the summer of 1950, I was invited to work for Budge Beckman's father, who was a general contractor in Westfield, New York. I worked as a laborer on some tank buildings and was even permitted to help design a small house for a client of the contractor. The Beckmans and their two grown sons allowed me to live and take my meals with them, and to hang on to all of my laborer's wages. The family knew that I had used up two of my GI Bill years and that less than half a year of college support was left.

I needed every penny of the money they had let me save when I returned to Raleigh in the fall. I rented a small basement room, lived frugally, and devoted myself full-time to my studies. My second-hand radio was my constant companion. Stuck for an idea one day, I took inspiration from listening to Stan Kenton's jazz to turn out a design project of which I was proud. I also discovered the Saturday Metropolitan Opera series, which took me home to the radio fare of my childhood. I listened intently and weekly during the season from that time forward, memorizing the music of the more familiar operas and identifying the voices of many of the stars.

Within a few months my GI Bill support ran out, and I took a part-time job in downtown Raleigh as a five-day-a-week draftsman for an engineer. I had bought an old car to take me from the campus to work, but my grades began dropping as study hours were forfeited to working hours. I applied for scholarship aid, but my grades and the fact that I operated a car worked against me. If I could afford to drive a car, I was told, I could afford the cost of school. I was awarded a scholarship of $100.00. Corresponding with the Clarks, I had obtained Jesse Miles' address in the States. I called him to borrow a small sum to get me through the semester, and he sent it to me. I finished up the year still working, and with lower grades.

The Clarks and I had kept in touch. Jean Clark wrote me occasional letters containing news of acquaintances and happenings in Buffalo. She had written me in the spring of 1948 about the birth of a third daughter, Peggy. From time to time she sent me pictures of the growing Clark daughters. She sent me a clipping and a note when Arthur assumed command of a reserve national guard regiment in New York in addition to his management duties in the family chemical plant. I wrote them about my activities, first as a soldier, then as a student. However, I did not return to Buffalo. It was not dislike that held me back, but pride. I wanted to live up to the confidence that both Clarks had shown in me when Arthur sponsored me to this country. I wanted them to see me as an immigrant-turned-American-citizen who had succeeded in carrying out his dream. They would be proud of me again, and justified in their decision to bring me here.

I had little else to do but try. I was beginning to comprehend that there was no replacing a family, and that forgetting one's family was more isolating than helpful. A family could give a man a starting point, a sounding board for ideas, inspiration for achievement, a refuge in times of need. One had to be deprived of his family to understand what being alone meant. I had to care about what I was doing. Who else would? By myself, I had to try to give meaning to my survival. Secretly I worked for my father's approval, fully realizing that I was holding to fantasy. My father had been reduced to ashes.

The Clarks had tried to help. Jim Pierce's family and the Beckmans had often invited me to their homes during school holidays. Others had invited me into their homes as well. But when the holidays were over, family members parted from one another attached by invisible strings as long as their lives, longer even. I left by myself, unattached. I found my own way and kept my own counsel. Often I lost my direction. Often I started over. Gradually, I became a part-time college student, part-time wage earner. I spent the early weeks of the summer of 1951 in Raleigh working for an ice show that came through town. I sold programs and flirted with the female ice performers. By the 4th of July, I was back in Washington, taking pictures of Harry Truman and members of his cabinet reviewing a traditional parade in honor of America's independence. I landed a job as a draftsman with the Agriculture Department of the Rural Electrification Administration, and continued to work through the fall, taking an elementary German class at George Washington University. I still thought of using my translating abilities, and wanted to improve my German grammar.

To relieve my loneliness and to attach myself to a group with whom I could find at least intellectual affinity, I occasionally attended services at the Unitarian Church. I chatted with various members of the church each week for companionship. I stayed away from synagogues and their congregations. And yet my mind, at times, was punctured with yearnings I wanted to stifle.

And so it happened that fall, while I was working in Washington, that I was seized with a strong impulse to attend Jewish New Year services. On the High Holy Days I joined a large Jewish throng in Constitution Hall, which served as a synagogue of adequate dimensions for the New Year congregation. The size of the crowd of worshippers frightened me, and the unfamiliar structure of the service disappointed me. I walked away still very much alone and still afraid to join a great Jewish herd. Even in Washington, D.C., my survival instincts had been aroused. Did I not know how readily such herds could be herded?

I continued to work days and study nights. When I had saved enough money, I returned to North Carolina State for another go at my architectural education. During spring semester, I received a notice from Washington, D.C., my stated permanent address, that I was to report to the Federal Courthouse to be examined for citizenship eligibility. I drove my jalopy up to Washington and proceeded to call on two old friends, Nick Satterlee and my former American history professor, to request their appearance as my witnesses at the courthouse the next morning. Then I called up a girl I knew and arranged to pick her up that evening as my date. My mood was ebullient, for tomorrow I would be a citizen. In the years since my arrival—months of confusion and homesickness to months of learning to stand on my own feet—I had acquired American habits. I now understood the freedom I had to become whatever I wanted, to seize or reject opportunities. Truly, I did not yet know what I would or could become, but I very much looked forward to assuming the privileges and responsibilities of American citizenship.

My elation, as I drove to pick up my date that night, outweighed my new sense of responsibility. The wail of a siren notified me that a motorcycle cop wanted me to pull over for speeding. I could not believe I had let myself be caught speeding the night before my citizenship examination

"Officer," I pleaded, as he started to write me a ticket, "if you give me that ticket I will not be able to be sworn in as a citizen tomorrow, and I am in Washington for that reason."

"What are you trying to tell me, buddy?" snarled the cop.

I explained that even one arrest on any count during the past years would automatically disqualify me from eligibility as a citizen. The cop accused me of being an artist at ingenious excuses, but enough doubt crossed his mind that he put his ticket book away and commanded me to follow him to a police station. There the police put their heads together to read ordinances and debate my point. They had not heard of such a law. A phone call to an attorney of the Department of Justice confirmed what I had told them. A misdemeanor arrest disqualified an applicant for citizenship. The cop tore up the citation.

"It's my gift," he said, "for becoming a citizen, but if I

catch you speeding tomorrow night, you're going to be one sorry citizen."

The next day my friends met me, as promised, at the courthouse. They laughed over the story of my close call and kidded me that they did not believe my jalopy could run fast enough to get me into such trouble. Inside, an interrogator questioned me on points of American history. My witnesses signed affidavits in my behalf. On April 8, 1952, I joined a number of other immigrant petitioners in a courtroom to be sworn in as an American citizen. I called the Clarks in Buffalo to tell them that I had become a citizen that morning and to thank them for bearing the long-term responsibility of sponsoring me in this country.

"How does it feel to be an American?" Arthur asked.

"I don't really feel much different except that now I'm able to do one thing I could not do before," said I in a mood to josh with him.

"What's that, Max?"

"When I get back to Raleigh I'm going to write my congressman to demand that Marshall Plan aid be stopped and immigration curtailed. Let those damned foreigners take care of themselves!"

We both laughed. That afternoon I returned to school in North Carolina. When the ice show came through again, in early summer, I worked it once more until it closed. One of the girl skaters who lived in Chicago suggested that I could probably easily get a drafting job there. Why not try Chicago, I thought. I could not earn enough in Raleigh to get me through another semester of schooling, and Chicago might be an interesting alternative to Washington.

I drove the girl to her home in Chicago, and found a job within a few days with Rand McNally, the map maker. But cartography did not interest me, I soon discovered. The tracing and drafting work assigned me were without creative challenge. I quit, and soon found a job with a large architectural firm on Michigan Avenue, called Fugard, Burt, Wilkinson, and Orth. Among junior draftsmen I was on the bottom rung, but I was pleased with the experience I gained there as we worked on drawings for a large hospital. One of the draftsmen invited me for

Thanksgiving to his home, just as someone had invited me every previous Thanksgiving. The easy hospitality of American families to outsiders always amazed and disarmed me.

Chicago was a dirty, unappealing city, but in the summer of 1952 it became an exciting place for me to be when I managed to attend both the Democratic and Republican conventions there. I applied for and received permission from my office to quit work at 3:00 PM in order to attend convention meetings. My co-workers, Chicago residents, were astonished that I had been able to gain entry to the conventions when they could not; but, then, they had never been trained in the art of *Organisierung*. Learning that the Democratic convention would be headquartered at the Hilton Hotel, I had gone there one weekend to seek out an arrangements staff and to find out about admission possibilities. In the staff room I ran into an old fraternity friend from the house that had pledged me at George Washington. Even then he had been a page on the Hill. In Chicago, when I met him, he was a rising young force in the Democratic party, sent out to help organize the nominating convention. I asked him how I could get into the convention, and he supplied me with a South Carolina newspaper press pass. Later, as the date for the Republican convention rolled around, I snooped about for a way to get into that one. Joining the Young Republicans was my key. By volunteering as a part of a Young Republican contingent to welcome Eisenhower and Nixon, I watched the Republican convention as well.

As an accepted—if bogus—member of the press corps, I had driven my old car in a line of press cars behind a police escort right up to the convention entrance. Inside I had roamed the floor, studying candidate Adlai Stevenson, Democratic party leaders and congressmen, observing the maneuvers of the political process. With the Republicans some weeks later I did the same thing, and was impressed to get a close look at General Eisenhower, another American wartime leader to whom I felt I personally owed a great deal.

In 1952, I looked over the two conventions for first-hand

evidence of the party and the candidate most likely to maintain the balance of the legislative, executive, and judicial branches of our government. Such a balance, I believed, was the key to America's strength as a democratic nation. Thus I prepared myself for my first vote as a citizen in the upcoming November election, a responsibility I took extremely seriously.

I never did get back to school. I finished out a year's work in Chicago, then drifted to Florida in summertime where I had vague hopes of establishing residency with Jim Pearce's family and of finishing my architectural education at a Florida state school. Jim's family was in no position to take me on as a long-term resident, however, and so I took a cabin on a beach and worked as a draftsman for a small-office architect there. The heat and humidity drained me, the drafting work was not stimulating, and I became discouraged. I called my old friend, Jesse Miles, who had become a colonel and was living in Indiana, for advice. When he invited me up for a visit, I packed up the jalopy and left as abruptly as I had arrived.

Once again I found myself crossing the country from South to North. I drove, as always, very fast and with assurance, tailing slower cars, awaiting that moment when I could pass. My reflexes were good as I worked at out-thinking and out-maneuvering other motorists. I drove through vast farmlands, small towns, over mountains and plains. I saw a country that consisted of many cultures and vastly differing communities. Yet, no matter how far I drove, I talked with people in one language only, even though we spoke to one another in a variety of accents. There seemed to be a thread of understanding that tied them all together. On the car radio I listened to our new president, Eisenhower, speak about sharing nuclear isotopes for peaceful purposes with all the peoples of the world.

Colonel Jesse Miles was teaching ROTC at the University of Indiana in Bloomington. He had married Ruth, a European girl he had first met in Bavaria, and whom I remembered well. I badly needed to talk to these old friends who knew who I was and where I had come from.

During my years in the States I had experienced many highs and lows: sometimes feeling that nothing could hold me back from becoming an architect and contributing useful and harmonious buildings; just as often feeling alone and unwanted, certain I would never design anything that would be built, and barely able to get through a day. At the time I visited Jesse and Ruth I was in one of my low moods. I was almost thirty years old. The money I had earned working was never enough to allow me a year of schooling at a time. I felt tired and very much alone. I told Jesse I had decided to give up on architecture and to reenter the army as a career soldier. I could put in my twenty years, be pensioned off at 49, and spend my old age sunning myself.

Jesse and Ruth were sympathetic, and they did not discourage my new resolve. Miles, a West Point graduate, had always taken pride in his career of service to the country. If I had bitten off more than I could chew, he was able to vouch for the satisfactions of an army career. The Korean War was in full swing, and having the option to take a year of military schooling before assignment to two years of active duty, I applied for and was admitted to Russian language studies at the Presidio of Monterey, California.

1953—1954

I took the train from Chicago to Oakland, California, dozing and dreaming as the train rolled through long, flat stretches of rich farmland. The train entered dry prairie lands, such as I had never seen, then began a slow upward climb into rugged mountain country that was both exciting and frightening to look upon. The train snaked its way down from the mountains to arrive in Oakland on the

California coast almost three days after departure from the central United States. The length of the country from Chicago to the West Coast stunned me.

At Oakland, I took a morning ferry to San Francisco, where I was to connect with a train to Monterey. Crossing the water toward San Francisco in fog, I could not see her modest downtown skyline or beckoning hills of white residences. The fog persisted that day, but my train did not leave until evening, giving me plenty of time to fill. I walked about downtown, then took a bus tour of the city. What I could see of San Francisco enchanted me. I was in a European city again. Knowing that Monterey was no great distance from San Francisco, I resolved to come back often on my weekends off.

Five years had gone by since my discharge from the army, and by 1953, when I reenlisted, basic training was required of me all over again. I entered training camp at Fort Ord, California, near Monterey. There I maneuvered according to past experiences to avoid the more rigorous routines, and sold candy bars in the barracks to hustle a little extra money.

Following basic training, I began Russian study classes at the Monterey Army Language School. My classmates were a fairly intellectual group, above-average college boys who, like myself, preferred intensive language training in order to qualify for special assignment during the Korean War years. Vocabulary building, phraseology, and pronunciation were stressed. Our goal was to speak and understand passable daily Russian within eleven months. I studied hard to keep pace with my bright classmates, but the migraine headaches, which still plagued me from time to time, returned with intensity. I went to the infirmary to seek relief. Various drugs the doctors prescribed relieved my pain, but also knocked me out. I began to miss classes.

One afternoon I went to the infirmary to request a refill of the medicine prescribed for me, and was ordered to a mental health clinic at Fort Ord. At the clinic I was admitted by appointment to see a psychiatrist who was sitting at his desk, looking over my records. He began questioning me about the nature of my bouts of pain and disability. He wanted to know if I was having difficulty coping with school. I replied that I did not believe school was a problem except for the constant interference of migraine attacks. Why did I quit architecture, he wanted to know. I searched my mind: money problems, discouragement, I offered; and added that I had reasoned that I might be better off in the service because I was familiar with army life and wanted to make myself useful as a translator in exchange for obvious benefits of security. Apparently noting references in my papers to concentration camp survival, the doctor quickly pinned me down as a Jew. He asked me leading questions about my Jewish background. I tried to deny that I was a Jew, but found myself becoming quite upset. The interview ended unsatisfactorily. The doctor was not pleased with my attitude, but he renewed my prescription and sent me back to duty.

I got along with my classmates, who filled our barracks with classical music instead of hillbilly, who preferred games of chess or bridge to the reading of comic books. Yet I remained an outsider among these boys from solidly middle-class families, many of whom had lived in one town all their lives. Some of them were Jewish and sensed that I was a Jew. They would invite me to Friday-night services and kid me when I insisted that I was a Protestant, as my dog tag showed. They asked me why I had a concentration camp number on my arm. I answered that I had been imprisoned as a member of the underground, a story they did not believe.

My migraines steadily grew worse. The intensity of our weekday Russian sessions drained my mental and physical strength. My one ace-in-the-hole was my weekend enjoyment of the California coast and the towns of Monterey, Carmel, and San Francisco.

I had not succeeded in forgetting about my architectural training. In fact, I missed it intensely. I found the Monterey public library, and on weekends I often spent afternoons there reading architecture and art history books. One of the librarians, noticing my interest, told me that her husband was an architect. After that, we often talked, and one day she invited me to meet her husband and to see their home which he had designed. I was impressed with the architect's use of space in their low-budget, rustic home, and delighted to be able to exchange ideas and philosophies with this couple. Together we looked at examples of contemporary California architecture in Carmel and Monterey.

I met architects from both towns when my new friends invited me to attend a charter dinner meeting establishing a new chapter of the American Institute of Architects in that area. Frank Lloyd Wright, who came to town on occasion to supervise a major house he was building there, had accepted an invitation to speak at the dinner. I sat content among architects and listened to Wright speak. Afterwards many of us pressed around him to ask questions and listen to his answers. More to remind myself than him that I had once been an architectural student, I blurted that I had met him when, as a student at N. C. State, I had crashed an upperclassmen's party in his honor. Looking at me sharply, he asked me what I was doing in the army, but did not seem to comprehend my answer that I had joined the service because of the difficulty of raising money to finish my education.

Many a weekend I took a bus the few miles to Carmel-by-the-Sea, which was then a quaint and sleepy town, charming and inexpensive enough to attract writers, artists, and professional people in retirement. I even took a moonlighting job there for a couple of months as a weekend busboy in the dining room of La Playa Hotel.

One Friday, when I heard some of my classmates were driving to San Francisco for the weekend, I jumped at the chance to join them, and we toured the town that night after our arrival. I awoke to a sunny Saturday morning and set off by myself to see as much as I could of San Francisco. I fell under the spell of a sparkling white harbor city built into the hills around the bay. The climate, the size, the shipping activity on the water, the liberal spirit afloat, reminded me of Amsterdam. I heard many languages spoken as I walked through downtown neighborhoods. I saw Italians, Chinese and Japanese, Mexicans, Filipinos, and Indians living and working without strife beside Russians, Irishmen, Germans, and black Americans. I discovered the opera house in the fall opera season. I became a weekend commuter to San Francisco, and a volunteer usher at the opera house in order to see as many operas as possible.

I slept nights at a YMCA Hotel on Turk Street, and began attending the Unitarian Church on Sunday mornings. There I met and talked with a woman, Anne Chamberlain, who then invited me to her Gough Street apartment for Sunday supper, and introduced me to her sister, Mary. The sisters belonged to a large family who were long-time residents of Berkeley. One weekend they invited me to Berkeley and introduced me to their entire family at their parents' handsome turn-of-the-century home. The parents and a number of their offspring were teachers and musicians. One son was a practicing architect. They were a warm and interesting group, and I enjoyed being included as a guest within their circle of friends. To my surprise I met there another old friend from George Washington University who, at that time, was stationed at Fort Baker as an adjutant to the commander.

In the ninth month of my schooling at Monterey I suffered a nervous breakdown. I had been given strong medication for a severe migraine and was lying semiconscious on my cot when my bunkmates began a routine "GI party", that is, a vigorous housecleaning of the barracks prior to inspection and the issuing of weekend passes. Awakened by the noise around me, I flew into a rage, jumped up and began overturning furniture, throwing objects around, and tearing up anything I could destroy. With enormous strength I fought and screamed as some of the GI's tried to pin me down. Eventually I was subdued. Some orderlies wrestled me into a straitjacket and onto a stretcher, then took me by ambulance to the "psycho ward" in a Fort Ord army hospital. There I rested in bed for a couple of weeks, visited daily by a young psychiatrist assigned to help me.

The psychiatrist asked me for a complete history, poking over details of my life I had almost forgotten. My youth and details of why I ended up in a concentration camp were of great concern to him. I tried telling him that my parents had died in bombing raids and that I had been caught and imprisoned by the Nazis while working with the Dutch underground, a story I thought I had been getting by with quite successfully. The doctor asked me if I had been raised a Jew, and I denied it. He was tenacious. At one session he informed me that he knew that Amsterdam had never been bombed. At another, I learned that the psychiatrist who had seen me earlier had filed a report alerting my commander to expect my breakdown at any time because of unresolved inner conflicts relating to my identity.

I soon realized that I was not going to be allowed out of the psychiatric ward until I opened up to the doctor, who was, after all, a sincere and likable fellow. With nothing to do but lie around and await his visits, I began to relax and decide to cooperate with him. I told him about my early life and background. I told him about my concentration camp experiences from those of a starving forced laborer, to hospital convalescent, to privileged member of the Paketstelle, to subhuman laborer again. I talked with him about my reasons for rejecting my Jewish heritage and my hopes for the future, which included more talk about architecture than a career in the service. Proudly I pointed out to him all that I had done by myself in the United States. A European working class boy obtaining a college education and almost completing architectural studies was an accomplishment that I was not sure the doctor could appreciate. I was beginning to describe the army once more as a way-station, and probably a mistake, but at least it was a way for me to earn and save some money, and I emphasized that I was continuing my education, even here, increasing my language skills.

By the time I was admitted to the general ward and permitted to walk to the doctor's office for our frequent "mental health" sessions, the psychiatrist was encouraging me to get out of the service as a first step toward mental recovery. I was frightened because I thought he intended to get me discharged on a "Section 8," or "psycho" discharge, which could jeopardize my future by severely limiting my chances at worthwhile employment. The psychiatrist explained that I could separate from the service with a general discharge because of medical findings, and that it would carry no psychiatric or other liabilities into the civilian world. However, I would no longer be eligible for service in the armed forces. He advised me to seek further psychiatric help after my discharge and to return to school to complete my architectural studies.

I promised the doctor that I would see a psychiatrist when I left the service, but confessed that I felt too old to return to school I relied on the words of one of my professors at N.C. State who had advised beginning students that those who could get through the first two years of architectural education could probably get through the rest. If a student could master the basics of the first two years, the professor had said, he would probably have little trouble getting through the next three years of expansion and embroidery upon basic knowledge. This expansion and extension of knowledge, I reasoned, could probably also be learned in architect's offices. I made up my mind that I would settle in San Francisco and that I would work in architect's offices and take night courses until I had gained the additional knowledge and experience necessary to take the California state licensing examinations.

In short order I was mustered out of the army. By terms of the general discharge I was asked to turn in my army uniform and, in its place, I was issued a civilian suit in my size, along with my mustering-out pay. Carrying with me a certificate of general discharge from the army under honorable conditions and a referral to the outpatient psychiatric clinic at Mount Zion Hospital, I arrived by bus in San Francisco in July of 1954.

My San Francisco friend, Anne, helped me find a small, first-floor studio apartment in a Taylor Street building on top of Nob Hill. A pull-down wall bed was the only furniture in the place besides some ancient kitchen appliances, but I was pleased with the hilltop location, and that first evening I went out to explore my new neighborhood. Night had fallen as I walked back to my apartment past little Huntington Park in the next block. Suddenly I was stopped in mid step as a man jumped from behind a bush and threatened me with a knife. His eyes were bloodshot and he appeared drunk but determined as he demanded my money. In my pocket was my mustering-out pay and my small savings, the only money I had. I looked at the man for no more than a moment, then sprinted off as fast as my legs could carry me for my apartment. I fumbled, sweating, to unlock the door with my key, and, as it turned in the lock, I glanced back. The man was nowhere in sight. I guessed he had been too startled by my reaction to chase me. Back in my apartment, however, I lay on my bed shaking for a long time before I calmed down enough to fall asleep.

The next morning I began my rounds of architects' offices. Before the week was out, I found myself a job as a draftsman.

PART 6

TAKING ROOT

I

Decades have passed since Arthur and Jean Clark sponsored me to this country. The opportunity their generous act gave me was the first step in a long climb toward a better life that millions of immigrants like myself have taken. The American dream, I was to learn, is as varied as the people who seek it, and as valuable as the effort put into realizing it. When I first arrived, I thought America owed me a living because of the injustices and suffering I had been through. My head had been full of misguided ideas. America, after World War II, was exploding with prosperity, creative vitality, and social revolution. At the time that I was wandering the country seeking my identity and my fortune, the GI's of that war were raising what was probably the most privileged generation of young adults to have yet been born. They were the beneficiaries of their parents' dream.

Taking prosperity for granted, postwar generations have come down hard on America's shortcomings, but they have also helped bring about some significant social changes, such as the advancement of civil and human rights, since the time I arrived in this country. During these years all of us have been profoundly affected by continuing domestic and international ferment, by political murders and scandals. America's "failures" have been identified and damned throughout the world, thanks to our habit of open self-criticism and to our free press. We have debated and fought over various emerging issues, but as a result we have also worked hard to make our system more justly responsive to our varying needs.

I cannot stand on the side of our country's detractors. From what I have observed and experienced, Americans possess a high degree of good will and balance, a balance that is possible for a people to achieve who have some say in their own destiny and who are not ultimately after power. Americans will always work toward change and reform, but because they prefer their individual and collective freedoms to power building, they will probably continue to swing away from radical manipulations. Perhaps because of their immigrant backgrounds and their common experiences with becoming self-reliant, Americans are quick to help others stand on their own feet. They will help immigrants, disaster victims anywhere in the world, the poor, and the handicapped, but after they have provided a minimum standard of security, they will back off. Each needy one is expected to learn to master his own destiny rather than to be mastered by the rescuers.

What America gave me and all of us when we came to this land, was an opportunity to shape our own lives. What we have done with that opportunity has been up to each of us. In one sense, each of us immigrants has become a pioneer in the same style as the American forefathers. They staged a revolution in the name of life, liberty, and the pursuit of happiness. Thanks to my American liberators, when I came to this country I had life (knock wood). I had liberty (and it was scary). Happiness I could not start chasing fast enough. Opportunity was one thing. Finding my way was another. Years of trial-and-error effort and loneliness lay ahead. Today I have to thank the Clarks for allowing me my own crack at the American scene. My dream has grown in scope from what it was when I arrived. It includes love of family, love of my tribe and heritage, love of this country that allows her varied millions to live and work peacefully in an ever-changing but ever-opening society; it includes the satisfaction of learning my capabilities, and that they can be expanded infinitely.

II

At thirty, in San Francisco, I began to come to terms with myself. In 1954, I signed on as a draftsman in whatever architectural offices needed a hand. The end of a project often meant the end of a job for me, and on I would move, to another office. After some months of drifting about, I settled into the office of Harry A. Thomsen in the last years of his practice before retiring. He had designed a number of San Francisco's post-earthquake, downtown buildings before the influx of new architects after World War II. Mr. Thomsen gave me my first projects to see through in their entirety from the planning and design stages to working drawings, and supervision of construction. He also granted me time off for weekly sessions with a psychiatrist, which continued for almost a year. I consulted with a doctor from the Mt. Zion psychiatric clinic, who was not only in possession of my Fort Ord records, but was Jewish himself. We faced one another over my problems, which to me meant my migraines. My breakdown was behind me, and I was heading once more in a direction I liked. To the doctor my problems were viewed as somewhat more complex, apparently, because he tried to steer me toward the dangerous territory of my rejected Judaism. This was upsetting. I pointed out that I had always had migraine headaches, even as a child, and that my mother and other relatives on her side had suffered them as well. Nevertheless, he felt there was a link between the present intensity and frequency of my headaches and some inner conflicts that I wanted to suppress.

In one interview the doctor brought up anti-Semitism, and I was shocked that he might see my turning from Judaism as anti-Semitic. No, doctor, I was not anti-Semitic. Almost crying with frustration, I groped for reasonable words of explanation. The problem, doctor, was fear, fear of anti-Semitism, and fear for good reason. Why should I subject myself and the offspring I hoped to have one day to such agonies as I had already experienced as a Jew. The religion did not mean that much to me that I must be prepared at any time to martyr myself over it. I had the same privilege of choice as everyone else, and I had made that choice. To think upon the history of the Jews was to remember long Sephardic laments that used to resound through our Portuguese Synagogue, recalling the sorrows and losses of centuries of anti-Semitism. I did not understand why people hated Jews, but I had no reason to doubt that they did, and I, for one, wanted out of that exhausting identity. And so we talked about this and all manner of things.

I kept busy as a volunteer night-and-weekend usher at the opera house and two downtown theatres. In my apartment I experimented with Buckminster Fuller's concepts of space-framing, using colored toothpicks as struts, then turning out a three-dimensional Christmas tree that, to my surprise, won some design publicity. "Manual therapy," my friends called my puttering.

One morning I awoke with chills and fever, and could not get out of bed. The doctor I called in to examine me diagnosed my illness as severe flu. Since I had no one to shop for or help me, the doctor arranged for me to enter Mount Zion Hospital, where he was on the staff.

I recuperated for a number of days in a primarily Jewish institution. Doctors and nurses talked and joked with me as one Jew to another. The other patients I met on the floor were mostly Jews and treated one another sympathetically and familiarly. Some of them ordered Kosher meals. The hospital seemed like home, and I was overcome with the realization of how homesick I had been. The day the doctor discharged me, I cried, and a nurse squeezed my hand and told me to visit the hospital staff any time I wished.

At my apartment I cried some more. Gradually, tears of frustration became tears of relief. My uncontrolled emotions surprised me. I wanted—I needed—to live openly as a Jew again. My desire to hide had dropped away. A great weight that had exhausted me was lifted. I wanted to proclaim to the world my Jewish heritage. I started by visiting Anne Chamberlain and confessing that her Unitarian friend, Max, was actually a Jew who wanted to live from that day forward as a Jew. I told her about my Jewish upbringing as the true reason I had been sent to the camps. I described how I had resolved, when I came to this country, to shed my Jewish past, but how I had suffered and been isolated as a result. Anne listened sympathetically and advised me to call a rabbi. When I did, the rabbi said, in effect, welcome back, and don't feel badly. Come to temple on Saturday to reacquaint yourself with your people.

I began attending a conservative temple regularly each week, and at some point during this period of return and rebirth, I stopped seeing the psychiatrist. My headaches had continued intermittently, and the psychiatrist had advised me that I would probably have to learn to live with them.

I was attracted to a girl I met at services, and began to visit her often at her apartment, where she lived with her mother. Within a few months I became engaged to her, then, disastrously, realized that I did not love her or share much in common with her. I was also realizing that attending temple every week was becoming a chore, and was no ready cure for past mistakes and present pains. With a sense of guilt and failure that made me physically ill once more, I broke the engagement, and at the same time began to slip in temple attendance.

Nevertheless, I was a Jew and no longer inclined to hide it. I had failed to lose myself in weekly ritual, but that did not change my Jewishness. My parents had not been devout, but they had lived as Jews and they had died as Jews. They had never experienced the shame, the self-disgust, that denying one's heritage can bring.

Behind me were years of bleak loneliness in America. Some stretches had been so awful I had almost wished I had not survived. I had lived a lie and been isolated by it. The defeated Nazis had continued to triumph over me and to keep me little more than a terrified survivor in spite of my efforts at accomplishment. Finally, I could respect myself once more. My destiny was that of a Jew. I embraced it. I looked forward to it. I could admit to myself my pride in the accomplishments of my people, and my love for them.

Down the ages of history the Jews had often been persecuted mercilessly for their religious noncomformance. With depressing regularity, in one place or another, they had been deprived of their livelihoods, their property, their lives. No matter where they were driven, these same people managed to retain their identity. Centuries of persecution have made the average Jew acutely interested in legal rights and humanitarian policies. Individually and as a group the Jews have directed great energy and intelligence toward human welfare. Some work for the down-trodden. Some elevate the arts. Some sharpen the sciences. Many sell and trade, thereby creating jobs and spreading prosperity. Others teach, or entertain, or practice in the law, government, philosophy, business. Very few are scoundrels. Most seek a better life for their communities and their families. How could I not be proud of my fellow Jews.

In 1954, I also discovered inviting delicatessens, kosher meat and poultry stores, and an outstanding Jewish bakery on McAllister Street in the heart of a Jewish ghetto (all since torn down and redeveloped for low-cost housing). I was drawn to McAllister Street each week as by a magnet. The odors and the sight of the foods displayed in the shops overwhelmed me as I mingled with Jews who shopped and window-shopped alongside me. I stuffed my tiny refrigerator with salamis, lox, chickens, and kosher dills I had bought, much of which had to be thrown away before I could get around to trying them. The dietary laws were not at the bottom of my enthusiasm, for I relished all kinds of foods, but I had a particular appetite for Jewish foods, even those that we Dutch Jews had never tasted.

At the office and among friends I told Jewish anecdotes and jokes to anyone who would listen. My joking sometimes angered intellectual friends who were offended by "ethnic" jokes, whose educated strivings stood in the way of their laughing at the human condition. I was no longer afraid of prejudice. It existed in America as it did in Europe. I accepted the existence of prejudice, but not the silencing of Max Garcia for expressing himself as a Jew.

I wrote the Portuguese synagogue in Amsterdam to inquire if any of my relatives had returned. Eventually I learned that five cousins lived: brothers Flip and Appie de Lara and Hans Rubens lived in Amsterdam with their three wives; Floortje Melkman had remarried (her first husband had died in the Holocaust) and had emigrated to Milwaukee, Wisconsin. I assumed that Meyer Hekster still lived—the older cousin who had left for South Africa in the early thirties—but I did not know how to get in touch with him. These five cousins, two of them brothers, were children of four of my mother's sisters: Klaartje, Grietje, Duifje, and Jetje.

I called Floortje on the telephone in a state of high excitement. She was shocked to hear from a cousin she believed to be dead, but we were soon chatting joyfully with one another. Impulsively, I told her I would fly out for a visit that weekend. I knew I did not have the money for the trip, and, indeed, that I rarely managed to save anything, but lived from paycheck to paycheck. My friend, Anne, admitted to having a little extra cash, however, and she lent me my airfare. I flew to Milwaukee for an emotional reunion with Floortje, her Dutch husband, Joep Hony, and their daughter, Anneke, at their apartment. Floortje, remembered as a happy girl growing into a carefree teenager as the war began, had matured into a pretty but anxious woman. For two days the three of us adults flooded the apartment with tears and words about what we had been through. Floortje described her lonely life in hiding during the war. Her grief over the loss of her family and first husband was such that their deaths might have happened the week before. Time had erased nothing. We exchanged stories and shared remembrances. We vented our bitterness over the families we had lost and our helplessness to bring any of them back. But talking together, one person to another who had suffered the same wounds, was balm of sorts. I left Milwaukee a relieved man to have been able to talk about relatives and friends to a living cousin who shared my ties with them.

I wrote my cousins in Amsterdam. We, too, exchanged pictures and news about what had happened to each of us. Flip and I corresponded the most frequently because we had once been the closest in companionship among my living cousins. I, alone, was unmarried.

In San Francisco, I continued to live as I always had, making friends by intuition and common interests. I found many Jewish friends, but I did not seek out a community of solely Jewish friends. Indeed, I was pleased that San Francisco Jews lived like Amsterdam Jews of my remembrance, as well-integrated citizens of the town.

In 1956, I married a Protestant girl, Priscilla Alden Thwaits, called Pat because of her initials. I met Pat on the rooftop of the Nob Hill apartment building in which we both lived, she on the top floor, I on the bottom. She was sunning herself and enjoying the view on a clear spring day. I was hanging up my socks to dry. Before the afternoon was over I lent her my volume of Andre Malraux's *The Voices of Silence*. A few years after her graduation from Middlebury College in Vermont, she had left her Plandome, Long Island, home and her public relations job in New York with *Newsweek* to live and work in the West. She had spent two years in New Mexico, and lived and worked in San Francisco almost a year before I met her. Living in the same building, I visited her often, enjoying her company and many of her interests. I invited her on excursions to see art museums and galleries, and to look over examples of Bay Area architecture. She divided her free time between me and a few tennis-playing friends of hers who shared her enthusiasm for that sport.

We spent many hours talking, and she questioned me, uncomprehending at first, about my history. She was pleased to hear me tell of finding my way back to Judaism, but, later, when I talked of marriage, she refused the idea of conversion in order to marry. She knew little about Judaism, she reminded me, and she believed that sharing a common religion was insufficient reason for marriage. Recalling my broken engagement, I did not push the point.

We were married by a San Francisco judge in a civil ceremony. Our honeymoon was spent visiting first her family and friends on Long Island, then my surprised "family": Arthur and Jean Clark in Buffalo, and Floortje and Joep Hony in Milwaukee. In San Francisco, Pat accompanied me to services whenever I attended them, and began familiarizing herself with Judaism through reading, observing, and asking questions. She also met my Jewish friends. From the time our first child, a son, was born, she wanted him to be raised a Jew. After all three of our children were born, she studied with a rabbi of the reform congregation we had joined, and converted to Judaism. Pat came to Judaism of her own volition. Even if by heritage she could not be Jewish, or, by nature, reject her own heritage, she hoped her family would want to live as Jews and to stand in the places of some of those Jews lost to fascism's "final solution."

We had few possessions when we married, but from the day we took our vows we felt wealthy. Life was a celebration. We bought paintings, ceramics, and plants before we bought washing machines and dishwashers. We bought books, and I set up a drafting and study room in a large walk-in closet of the first apartment we rented. I filled our three rooms with flowers and brought my wife candy and pastries on weekends, just as my father had brought to my mother whenever he could afford it.

By the time our first child, David Alden Rodriguez Garcia, was born in 1957, ten months after we were married, I was spending long evening hours hunched over my books or in classes, preparing for my state boards in architecture. Shortly after the birth of our second child, Tania Sippora Alden Rodriguez Garcia, in 1960, I received my California license. My wife called me at the office I worked to read me my license number. I told her that I could die on the spot a satisfied man that I had achieved my childhood goal. She laughed and remarked that my childhood dream might be fulfilled, but my life's work had just begun.

Several months later I applied to the Hebrew Free Loan

Association, about which a friend had told me, for their small maximum loan in order to start a business. Hebrew Free Loan officials informed me that they had not lent money to anyone before for the purpose of starting an architectural practice, and they considered me a risk. However, they accepted my application and the signatures of four underwriters as collateral, and lent me $2,000.00, interest free. I had lined up some kitchen remodelings, room additions, and a house for a family of six in the hills of Marin County. One room of the Jackson Street Victorian flat we had moved to became my office-drafting room. Pat took on my secretarial work. We earned enough to pay the rent, increments on our loan, and save a little. In the following spring of 1961, our third child, Michelle Rozetta Helen Alden Rodriguez Garcia, was born. Our flat was looking more like a nursery than an architect's office. I rented office space in a building on Mission Street, and moved my practice downtown.

I had about seven years of work in architectural offices behind me when I opened my own office in 1960. I thought I knew how to run an architectural practice, and, indeed, I had gained good experience in almost every phase except one important one: selling my services to clients. No sooner was I licensed than I started a practice. Looking back, I have to laugh at my audacity. But I was thirty-six years old, and a man who had fought hard for the privilege of life. The risk of starting a practice had not seemed all that great. We had children. We had no savings in the bank and no backlog of wealthy friends waiting to engage my services for building projects. To be sure, Pat's family helped in the early years. Aunts and uncles and sister and brother-in-law commissioned variously a home-remodeling, a house, an office design. Pat's parents lent us another couple of thousand dollars when a client was slow in paying, and I could not otherwise pay my draftsmen. Locally, I followed up every remodeling, building, or planning possibility that I heard of. I believed I could sell my services and, somehow, I did. No project was too small for me to undertake. I relished the challenge of learning to design for small budgets, and of learning the necessity of carefully detailed working drawings and specifications. The first years of practice were difficult. I brought in a miscellany of small budget jobs, but no matter how much time I gave my clients or how well a project turned out, the prestige work always went to better known architects. Some nights my wife and I hardly slept wondering how we would get through the next month. If I became discouraged and talked of teaching or going back to work for someone else, Pat encouraged me to continue, reminding me of the pride I took in seeing each project through. Sometimes the shoe was on the other foot, and I would have to convince my wife that the practice could yield a decent living to take care of the needs of our growing family. Luckily, neither of us were ever of a mind to quit at the same time. Often on weekends, however, we would put our cares aside, entertain our friends, and laugh. We liked what we were doing and we felt good about life.

For its population, San Francisco attracts a disproportionately large number of architects. I competed for commissions with established firms and a mushrooming number of new practices. For the first five years, I worked on residential and small commercial remodelings, additions, and new buildings. I designed individual homes for middle-class families in the early sixties when such homes were feasible. Gradually, I developed a clientele in commercial and corporate work, and some luxury custom homes. The size and number of the projects grew. There were many satisfactions. There were also some tough lessons that were blessings in disguise. The more I learned about the business of architecture, the better I could handle the bigger and more complex projects that came with time.

From the start I took great satisfaction in being able to support my family by doing work that I had always wanted to do. At first, draftsmen were hired only intermittently. Later, I learned the responsibilities of employing a steadily-expanding, full-time staff. In time, key staff people emerged who have helped develop an efficient team operation. I continue to put in many hours of effort seven days a week, but I rarely look upon the practice as work. In truth, I am delighted to be paid for spending my time so agreeably.

Our son, David, and our daughters, Tania and Michelle, transformed our lives, making each day meaningful, giving us strength we did not know we had. We were pleased to become parents, to love and interact with our children, to help and be helped by them. We disciplined and taught them according to what each of us had learned, and, at times, ours must have been conflicting messages. In no time at all, the children began teaching us, bringing us in touch with their generations of the American young. We worked to give them security and opportunities to develop themselves. They rewarded us with astonishing growth and a variety of abilities. Our home filled up over the years with their friends, hobbies, pets, musical instruments, and sporting equipment for every season. As each child reached school age, he or she began public school on the weekdays and religious school on weekends. David celebrated his Bar Mitzvah at the age of 13. One by one, all three children were confirmed at our temple.

Nine years after I opened an office, I bought a comfortable Edwardian house for our family. As American houses go, it is old, but even after building or remodeling various luxury homes for clients, buying a spacious older home for my family's use seemed foolhardy. How could I be sure that my practice would not falter? Once my debts of earlier years had been repaid, I had vowed never to borrow money again, and I had not. Buying a home meant a mortgage and taxes in addition to office overhead. For me, home ownership was uncharted territory, a luxury beyond our needs. For Pat, it was a way of life. She was used to property and a surplus of seldom-used rooms. She thought the children would thrive in a home of their own. I thought they were thriving anyway. We had our first bitter quarrel over the need for a house. Pat argued that the practice was well-established and that regardless of ups and downs in the economy, home ownership would prove cheaper and more beneficial than rental. I looked at the scale of interest rates and was not convinced. My wife won that one, and I have never regretted her talking me into buying our home.

We have corresponded with the Clarks every year, but because we are at opposite ends of the country, we have seen little of each other. In 1968, however, Arthur and Jean brought Barbara and Peggy, then college girls, through San Francisco on a touring trip. They joined us for drinks at our Jackson Street flat, then dinner in Chinatown. Our three young children accompanied us and met the Clark family for the first time. The Clarks had recently taken a Florida home, where they had begun to spend their winter months, far from the frigid winds and snows of Buffalo.

Arthur and I reminisced about the early days of our meeting at the end of the war. Neither Arthur nor I knew much about former associates. We no longer knew where Colonel Jesse Miles was. A few years previously we had both been invited to a reunion of a few members of the 319th Infantry Regiment whom former Captain Salomone had somehow tracked down. Salomone had sponsored the reunion at the Plaza Hotel in New York, of which he was then the manager. Clark had not been able to attend, and I had not been able to afford the trip. Years later I managed to find Jesse Miles, and to reminisce with him by phone about the course of our lives since we had seen one another last in 1953. I was surprised to hear that he, Salomone, and a few other members of the 319th still got together from time to time. Jesse and his wife, Ruth, had also retired to Florida, but were unaware that the Clarks had a home there too.

We have visited with members of my wife's large and far-flung family on a number of occasions, or they have visited us. We have kept in touch with Floortje Hony and Appie and Hans de Lara. Jim Pearce, my University of Washington friend, settled in San Francisco soon after Tania was born. He has remained a family friend and much-needed "uncle" to our children through their growing years.

At about the time of my marriage, Anne Chamberlain's sister, Mary, had also married; and she and her husband left soon thereafter on a European trip. As a favor to me, they called on Flip and Appie de Lara and their wives in Amsterdam. Not long after their visit, I was shocked to receive two letters within a two-year period informing me that first Flip, then Hans Rubens, had been killed in separate automobile accidents. My Amsterdam relatives were narrowed to Appie de Lara and his wife, Hans.

III

From time to time Pat asked me about what I remembered of Amsterdam and if I ever missed my native country. She was disappointed that I did not teach our children Dutch, not even a few phrases, not a Dutch song. Occasionally, I had told her a little about my childhood in Amsterdam, but I maintained that I disliked any thought of Holland. There were too many painful memories. Dutch was a language I had given up when I emigrated, and I did not intend to teach it to my children. The children were Americans. I tried to forget my native language and spoke it only when I talked by telephone with Floortje who spoke to me in Dutch during long, intimate conversations that were weighted with her unalleviated grief.

With the passage of time, however, I found myself secretly yearning to walk the streets of Amsterdam again. At times I had awakened from sleep unbelieving of some remembered scene or experience. Sometimes I awoke still a prisoner in the camps and convinced that everything that had happened to me since had been a dream. I could not relate my life in America to the life I had once lived. I said nothing to my family, but one day I surprised them with an announcement that we were all going to Europe where we would buy a car and tour many countries, including my country and my home town.

In 1971, twenty-five years after my arrival in the United

States, I took my family back to Europe. I drove them to Amsterdam and Antwerp to show them the places where I had lived. We drove down the familiar streets of my childhood where I easily found my old neighborhoods. I showed my family the apartment blocks in which I had grown up. The children caught my mood of joy and relief at finding the buildings still standing. I would have doubted everything I remembered had these structures disappeared. To my surprise, my children were able to understand my need to find again the world of my childhood, and they encouraged me to show them every evidence I could find of my living boyhood. One of the children remarked that I had lived in some very nice neighborhoods. I was proud that the neighborhoods I had once roamed in two different cities were "nice" even now. The tidy blocks of low brick apartment structures pleased me anew in their discreet detailing, in their unity and scale. We toured the old working and shopping neighborhoods, and looked at the old Asscher Factory. The Graaf Floris School had been changed to an administration building. In Antwerp the middle school (or junior high school) was still there, along with its awful memories of the school dentist.

Back in Amsterdam, I walked joyfully through the streets, showing my family what must have been for them a bewildering number of points of interest. I spoke Dutch eagerly with the Mokummers, sharpening my ability with each passing day. I introduced my children to the delights of swallowing smoked eel and fresh herring with chopped onion at open street stalls.

One luxury I had not been able to resist for my family was to treat them to two nights as guests at the Amstel Hotel. In my childhood, as now, the Amstel, at Sarphatiestraat and the Amstel River, was one of the finest hotels in town. I used to pass by on my way to and from the Jodenbreestraat, and watch the well-dressed guests come and go. On many an occasion I had run up the steps to peer through the doorway, only to be chased back down by an indignant doorman. It gave me great pleasure, therefore, before we left on our European trip, to reserve rooms for my family at the Amstel Hotel.

After touring much of Holland that I had never seen, I

nosed the car down to Germany and to my route through postwar Europe as a volunteer aide to two units of the American army. We retraced my travels through Bavaria, Czechoslovakia, and Austria, ending at Ebensee. We found the camp there, which had been reduced to a small memorial graveyard, barely marked and unobtrusive. To get to the camp, I had turned our car up a mountain road and through an arched gate that for me alone were familiar landmarks. Had it not been for the road and the gate, even I would have been lost. New housing, lawns, and gardens covered most of the old grounds. To one side was a small memorial graveyard. Gravestones and a few plaques along a memorial wall testified to the names and nationalities of a few of the political prisoners who had died there. Memorials to Catholic priests and political dissenters mingled with those of a great number of Jews. Behind the memorial wall, the crematorium chimney was still standing.

In Ebensee we stayed at the inn that had served as American headquarters for 3rd Cavalry Tanks during the early weeks of occupation. The place had been extensively remodeled, and I recalled for the startled innkeepers details of how it had once looked. I told them who I was, and asked how part of the old camp grounds could have become a graveyard inasmuch as I had witnessed the mass burials of dead prisoners along the roadside. They told me that the bones had been moved up to the memorial graveyard when it had been dedicated. We walked about and marveled at the breathtaking blue lake surrounded by emerald mountains. The resort appeared to have no dark secrets.

Wherever we drove as we retraced parts of my journey twenty-five years before, I talked with people about what I remembered. They discussed the occupation years with me with more introspective interest than reluctance to talk. At Aschaffenburg, where the 80th Division was processed for return to the States, a middle-aged woman innkeeper told me the story of how the Americans, when they invaded, had shelled the town from across the river, and of how she had managed to save her inn from the path of the shells. Scheinfeld Castle, where I had been stationed with the 18th Regiment, First Infantry, had been converted to a private girls' school. The headmaster invited my family to his house, where we talked for an hour. His daughter was married to an intern who had taken much of his medical training in the United States, and planned to settle in Colorado.

I talked to Germans and they talked to me. As a Jewish survivor of mass killings by the German state, I no longer felt qualms about presenting myself and my views to Germans. They had to deal with me, a Jew. I was back among them. I did not accuse them, but I recalled with them some things that were probably not comfortable for them to remember. If I had refused all intercourse with Germans, if I did not set foot in their country, I would be their victim still. I would be shriveled with my hatred. Some words of advice my father used to give his family have never left my memory. Forgive, my father advised us, but do not forget. I used to wonder about the how's and why's of those words. In the long run, his has been good advice. I bear no hatred for all Germans such as they once demonstrated toward Jews.

After the retracing journey, we traveled through many cities and countries in a high mood. I had warned my family as we had flown toward Europe that they would find that continent old-fashioned and slow-paced compared with what they were used to. I was the one to be surprised. The western European countries were booming, working at a frantic pace to produce and comsume on an American scale. Networks of highways had been built to accommodate the Europeans' new cars. Imaginative contemporary buildings mingled freely with ancient, traditional ones. The interiors of some classic buildings had been transformed to ultra-modern spaces. Shops and restaurants had multiplied. Self-service and self-expression were the new order of the day. The cities—each with its distinctive style and traditional flavor—bustled with new life. The regional foods were still delicious; the rolling, fertile countryside, a feast for the eyes.

Czechoslovakia, on the other hand, had deteriorated since the end of the war. Cities, towns, and farms were run down. I had missed seeing Prague in 1945 because the Americans would not risk my being picked up there by the Russians. I obtained visas for all of us to go there in 1971. We stopped at Marienbad (Marianske Lazne) and Karlsbad (Karlovy Vary) on the way. Quiet, sullen men and women took the waters in shabby surroundings that had once been beautifully maintained. The restoration of Prague's elegant but crumbling old buildings was just beginning, and progressing at a snail's pace as laborers worked with muscle power and wheelbarrows more often than with machinery and trucks.

Pat and I were appalled by the fascist style of their new architecture. People lived in walk-up apartments stacked like shoe boxes. It was evident that human proportion and scale had never been a consideration, nor were the amenities of living. The buildings were drab blocks, poorly landscaped, their dullness relieved only by the festive red of the ever-present communist flags draped from their sides. The red flags of the Communists lacked swastikas; otherwise, they reminded me of flag-draped buildings of the era of the Third Reich.

Seeing that we were Americans, first a woman, then a man, stopped us on the streets to complain to us in English or German about the conditions of their lives. They were bitterly opposed to their Russian masters, but felt helpless. Our children, who had thoroughly enjoyed western Europe, were anxious to leave Czechoslovakia, her unappetizing restaurants and shops, her endless restrictions, and machine-gun-toting border guards.

An important mission of the trip was to meet Appie de Lara and his wife, Hans, now my closest living relatives in Amsterdam. The two of them met me for the first time as an adult and, at the same time, began a cordial relationship with my family. Appie had picked up the shambles of his father's feather business after the war and had gradually built it into a substantial international trading firm. Hans was an active partner. The de Laras had two grown and married children and four grandchildren. The son, Michel, was a third partner in his father's business. The daughter,

Philika, took up medical studies while raising two young sons, and was to become a physician by 1976. Even though my cousin is almost fifteen years older than I, the two of us easily fell into a brotherly relationship. Our families remarked in amazement about our resemblance to one another. Hans seemed like my sister. Not only as Appie's wife, but as a fellow Mokummer and a survivor of Ravensbrück and Bergen-Belsen concentration camps, she and I had much in common. We began a long dialogue about survival that showed us how preoccupied we had become with that subject. In our subsequent visits to Amsterdam or theirs to San Francisco, the dialogue has continued and been joined by their grown children. Hans, who had repressed her memories of the concentration camps, found the ability to talk with me about her experiences and mine, and then with her whole family. She showed me a book about Ravensbruck camp, written by a former prisoner, in which she was mentioned for particular compassionate acts. But why, we ask ourselves, do we few survive all our dead?

We do not dwell always on grim subjects. More often, we pay tribute to our departed loved ones by laughing affectionately over remembered episodes in our lives with them. As we talk, we repopulate the streets of old Amsterdam with relatives and friends bustling about their daily chores. We pore through the de Laras' illustrated books about Amsterdam to verify details of our remembrances.

Appie, like Mrs. Klaverstyn, had been spared by the Nazis during the occupation because he had married a gentile. Hans had been born of a Jewish father, gentile mother, and raised a gentile. Ironically, it was Hans who had landed in a concentration camp, not as a Jew, but as a participant in the underground who was caught at her work of placing orphaned Jewish children in hiding. Since the war, the de Laras have raised a Jewish family, and their married children and grandchildren have maintained their Jewish heritage.

Before we left the United States I had arranged to attend

services at the Portuguese Synagogue to say kaddish for my parents and sister. To my amazement we met there a distant cousin, Appie Garcia, who I had not known was alive. He and his wife, Mimi, invited our family to join them and their two sons for dessert that evening. They invited his mother as well. I remembered her far better than I did Appie, who is several years younger than I. Appie's father, like mine, had paid little attention to religious observance. His own mother admitted that she was not devout. I was curious that Appie and Mimi kept a kosher household and attended the Portuguese Synagogue regularly. Appie explained to us how he had encouraged his family to become devout after he had begun to consider deeply what being Jewish meant. He had consulted the rabbi of his congregation to help him understand the significance to him, a contemporary Jew, of what is written in the Torah, the body of cultural, philosophic, and moral teachings that has guided Jews through the ages of their history. The six-day war of 1967, in which Israel triumphed over her Arab attackers, served to confirm for the Garcia family the importance of continuing the struggle to keep Judaism and a Jewish homeland alive.

The Garcias are one of a handful of families making up the active Portuguese congregation today. Appie gave me a copy of the Garcia family tree that traced our Sephardic ancestors back to South America, and before that to the Iberian Peninsula, where they lived until the Spanish Inquisition.

The grandmother, Appie and Mimi Garcia, and others of my family and friends, owed their survival to individual Dutch people who took it upon themselves to hide Jews, just as a family had tried to hide me. A number of Dutch people, I was proud to have verified, had assumed great personal risks to help Jewish fellow-citizens.

I tried to look up Mevrouw van der Roest, my primary school teacher, at her house, which is still standing. She was no longer there, nor could her name be found in the phone book. I would have liked to have seen her again and to have talked to her about what she remembered as our teacher in a classroom of Jewish and gentile children, many of whom were to disappear in the Holocaust.

During our travels, one of the cities in which our family stopped was Zurich, Switzerland, where the brother of a San Francisco friend of ours lives. I called the brother for my friend. He and his wife invited us to their house that night for coffee and dessert, mentioning that they had a houseguest. We were welcomed into their home in the hills above Zurich Lake and introduced to their houseguest, an older man from Johannesburg, South Africa.

"Silly of me to ask," I began as I shook hands with the Johannesburger, "but would you by chance know a man named Meyer Hekster? I believe he may live in or near Johannesburg."

"Meyer Hekster? If we are talking about the same man, we are talking about one of my best friends."

"Meyer Hekster?" It was my turn to question the name in astonishment. Together we established that we were, indeed, talking about the same Meyer, a man who had come from Amsterdam in the early 30's and established himself in the South African diamond industry. He was then near seventy years of age, I learned, and I obtained his address from his friend. Our little group who had barely met marveled that the two of us from widely separated parts of the world could know someone in common. Their guest's friend was my relative.

Shortly after our return to the States, I began exchanging news with Meyer and his wife, Eva, who lived in Cape Town. Their son, Ralph, was married, the father of three children, and a practicing dentist there. Some years later we received news that the entire family had left South Africa to return to Amsterdam.

On subsequest European trips, my wife and I have visited with the senior Klaverstyns—the parents of my childhood friend, Appie—who still live in a tiny but pretty apartment on Saffierstraat. It was Mrs. Klaverstyn who was able to tell me details I did not know of my mother's interest in attending operettas and of her unfulfilled passion for fine clothing. Mr. Klaverstyn reminisced with me about the days in the 30's when he, my father, and other Social Democrats fought in the streets with the Communists. Laughing modestly, he allowed that my father was the more active combatant in such encounters. In socialized Holland, Mr. Klaverstyn is still a Social Democrat, but he is proud of the accomplishments of his son in Australia, and enjoys their visits back and forth. He showed us an album of pictures of Appie's family and home in Australia. Just as our American older citizens, the senior Klaverstyns worry about increasing crime, the number and speed of passing cars, dirty streets, and the heedless pace of modern life. Their hospitality to my wife and me is in the gracious style of another day. As we chat, they offer us tea with cheeses, sausages, cakes, cookies, candies, and nuts.

Appie Klaverstyn moved to Australia soon after I saw him last at the end of the war. By mail, we have shared our remembrances of boyhood antics and former classmates at Graaf Floris Primary School. It was news that Appie, too, had an eye for the delicate blonde who occupied a rear seat in the row next to ours. We congratulate one another on how well we have raised families and prospered in the societies in which we live. We comment ruefully on the evidence of aging our latest photographs reveal to one another; yet we can still recognize the skinny, light-hearted buddies who were born a few days apart, and who sat near one another for six years in Mevrouw van der Roest's classroom.

We discuss our concerns over the struggle between the communist and democratic blocs of nations, for we both see communism and fascism as essentially the same wolf under different skins. A reunion of our grammar school classmates would be small indeed, and we do not forget why. We have reason to be wary of the wolf.

Visits and letters exchanged between relatives and boyhood friends: these have been the keys to the box in which I had locked away the memory of my heritage in order to survive. I no longer watch with envy my wife's easy intimacy with members of her family. As I grow closer to my own family, I also draw closer to hers. We all have much in common, we family people.

When we visit the de Laras in Amsterdam, Hans is delighted that I not only remember, but hanker after her Dutch cooking. After a day's work, Hans does not begrudge shopping and cooking for her American cousins. With enthusiasm we sit down to her enormous dinners, starting with a good soup, and ending, after many courses, with fresh pastries from a local bake shop. Hours later we munch candies, nuts, and fresh fruits. We talk endlessly and comfortably with one another. I try to remember to interpret for my wife. Sometimes Appie and I shout at one another, his Dutch viewpoint at angry odds with my American one. The storm passes. We laugh and joke and needle one another. We do not stop talking. What we say is often of little importance. Before we know it, the time is 2:00 AM. The de Laras plan to be at their office by 7:30 in the morning.

IV

Forgive, my father used to tell me, but do not forget. I have forgiven the German people. Toward which ones would I direct my vengeful anger and to what end if I dare hope that my children will live in a developing society. The perpetrators of incredible crimes against Jews have died or changed or slipped like sand through the fingers of pursuers.

The victims and the survivors themselves stand accused, in some widely read scholarly studies, of cooperating in their own destruction and of not resisting enough. As these criticisms pertain to Nazi-occupied Holland and to conditions of survival in the camps, I have found some basic misconceptions and inaccuracies. On these pages I have tried to set forth honestly my own experiences, reactions, and learning processes for the reader to evaluate. I came by my information first-hand. I lived through all the experiences I describe. Thus, it is difficult for me to read or listen to the opinions of scholars who were able to escape the eye of the storm about the individual or collective guilt of victims or survivors. The aim, I suppose, is to strengthen Jews to believe that such a catastrophe need never happen again, but from my point of view their lofty statements are made at the expense of victims and survivors.

Their reasoning seems wishful. We should have been ideal Jews, unified religiously with our entire people, realizing as a group that resistance would lead to many deaths but would also bring an end to persecution. Though holding to unique ties of religion and tradition, Jews are not above or beneath general human experience. Many are learned, but some are ignorant. Some are pious, some are not. Some are selfless in the service of God and mankind. Some prefer secular or selfish interests. Some are rich, some poor.

I can speak for the poor at the time of the Holocaust, such as my family. The story I have told is typical, I believe, of Jews who were caught in Europe without resources. In spite of postwar conjecture, all Jews did not know what was in store for them at the hands of the Nazis. Many would not believe such evil intentions toward them; and if they did, there was no place for them to go unless they saw the light very early in the game. Many Jews were bound by poverty and by family ties. Once they were netted and sent to the camps, they lived, if they were lucky, by their own will and by hope. Most camp victims were alone, and there was no beating the system. An uprising of the few meant death for many. Most of us prisoners were of poor enough stuff not to seek out martyrdom or the brief glory of the hero. So we bear the brunt of some accusations.

I, too, would like to hope that the lessons of the Holocaust have helped prevent the igniting of similar infernos, but our news sources tell us otherwise. (Even today in many countries of the world bloodbaths are underway; round-ups and imprisonments of "undesirable" citizens are taking place.) As for my survival, I refuse to bear guilt for it or for anything I had to do in the camps to survive. According to the will and the conscience of the boy I was then, I did the best that was in me.

I have forgiven much, and in so doing I have gained a great deal. It is also true that I do not forget. I am at one with myself as a Jew, content to be husband, father, and family member. I enjoy the practice of my profession and all the benefits of life in America, including the beauty of the city in which I live and to which I contribute my efforts. Still, I have not forgotten even for a day my uprooting in early life and my experiences in Nazi concentration camps. A remark, an incident, a dream—any of these things—can bring the camps sharply back into focus at any time. Even after seeing Ebensee, I begged Pat to go with me to Poland to see Auschwitz. An obsession to see Auschwitz gnawed at my mind. My wife had resisted. Ebensee had been enough, she said, and the recollections I had shared with her had supplied her with clear and believable insights into what life had been like in the camps. She had asked me what would be served by my seeing Auschwitz again, and I could not answer.

Back in 1975, Pat and I made the necessary pilgrimage to Auschwitz, a trip made no easier by travel conditions over the peasant-dominated roads of modern Poland. Our car trailed slowly over two-lane roads behind peasants walking or driving horsecarts, or riding bicycles or motorcycles. Supply trucks dominated the sparse motor traffic. We crawled through strings of their villages. Road signs to Krakow were not to be found. We carefully followed our map. Travel conditions were much slower than anticipated, and despite warnings against night travel, we arrived in Krakow after dark. A room at a good hotel for unexpected and unescorted visitors from America was coldly granted. Our passports were held at the desk until our departure after breakfast the next day. We set out for Auschwitz in a fine rain and arrived there by late morning.

The camp had been converted to a museum, and the museumlike quality of the preserved buildings all but obliterated the memory of the gaunt hordes of prisoners who once filled them. Knots of adults and throngs of Polish schoolchildren—most of them brought by bus—swarmed through the camps in small groups led by tour leaders. I got my bearings and led my wife on a tour of our own through the buildings and grounds.

The buildings were smaller and closer together than I had remembered them. Grass-covered courtyards and tall poplars lining the avenues of barracks buildings were amenities I did not remember. Some of the buildings preserved the original barracks arrangements: the brick or wooden bunk tiers, straw-filled, the *Blockalteste's* quarters; some, the hospital quarters. There were torture rooms, solitary dungeons, rooms I had not seen as a prisoner. A number of the buildings had been converted to memorial museums to commemorate various national groups who had died there. The Jews, too, were given museum space. We were moved by the Jewish memorial display of symbolic and traditional designs worked into glazed tile walls and highlighted by spotlights in a darkened room. More than any other element, however, the use of photographs brought the camp back to life. Blow-up shots of skeletal prisoners, taken while the camp was operative, were used effectively on the walls. The barracks hallways were lined with smaller identification photographs of shorn-headed victims. Their names, places of birth, and dates of death were recorded beneath the pictures.

We entered a small bookstore that had been built outside the main gate. Many books about the camp, Nazism, and related subjects, were offered for sale. Most were in Polish, but a number were offered with Russian, German, French, and English translations. The bookseller, a Polish man in shortsleeved shirt, bore a tattooed Auschwitz number older than mine on his left forearm. He was talking in German to a small group of students who were inquiring about his books; and, when he finished, I introduced myself in German as a former member of the camp and asked him if many other former prisoners came back to see the place. His face broke into a grin as he told me that many prisoners used to visit but fewer came back each year. So it isn't true that we who survived Auschwitz will never die again, I remarked; but I am not sure the bookseller understood my reference to a song we prisoners had once sung.

I bought some books and asked him where we could find records of the precise arrival and departure dates of my transports into and out of the camp. He directed us to a converted barracks building which he said housed the camp archives. We found the archives, but, to our great disappointment, we were turned away without explanation by the people working inside. Nearby, I listened to Polish school children exclaim in shock over their discoveries at the museum. I wondered how much they knew about Russian camps or the writings of men like Aleksandr Solzhenitsyn.

The "post office" was closed to the public, as was one of the infirmaries in which I had stayed. I showed my wife the kitchen building in front of which gallows had once been erected and used. The iron entry gate bearing the wrought iron legend, *Arbeit Macht Frei,* stood as I remembered it, with the whorehouse to the left as one entered the camp. My last impression was my first. I was astonished at how much smaller in scale everything was than I remembered it.

We did not stay for guided tours or to see confiscated Nazi films about the efficient operations of the death camp. We did not follow the crowd to view roomsful of victims' hair, clothing, glasses, and such. I did not need that kind of reminder. Touching back to this bitter ground, seeing that it did indeed exist, that the buildings, even if moderated, were still there—this evidence was enough for me. We did not stay long at Auschwitz. We paid a young boy our parking fee, then could not resist purchasing from his mother's souvenir booth a small, plastic Auschwitz pennant before we headed down the cluttered road to Czechoslovakia on our way to reaching Vienna that night. The rain continued to fall.

Typesetting and Layout by Noel and Anne Sosebee, New Market, Alabama; Printing and Binding by George Banta Company, Menasha, Wisconsin.